A Student's Guide
to Böll

STUDENT'S GUIDES TO EUROPEAN LITERATURE

A Student's Guide to Böll

by

ENID MACPHERSON
Head of the Department of German
South Shields Grammar School for Girls

HEINEMANN EDUCATIONAL BOOKS
LONDON

Heinemann Educational Books Ltd
22 Bedford Square, London WC1B 3AH
LONDON EDINBURGH MELBOURNE AUCKLAND
HONG KONG SINGAPORE KUALA LUMPUR NEW DELHI
NAIROBI JOHANNESBURG IBADAN
EXETER (NH) KINGSTON PORT OF SPAIN

ISBN 0 435 37576 8

Printed in Great Britain by
Spottiswoode Ballantyne Ltd, Colchester and London

Contents

to David

Foreword

This book is an introduction to the novels and short stories of Heinrich Böll. It is intended primarily for the student of German literature but should be of interest to all involved in the study of post-war literature. To this end, although quotations are given in the original German, translations have been included, in line with the general policy of this series.

Böll's critical essays and lectures have been examined in some detail since they throw much light on Böll, the creative writer, and quotations from them allow him to be, to some extent, his own commentator.

Page references to quotations are taken, for the most part, from the cheapest available paperback editions of Böll's work, readily accessible to the student: Series: *Deutscher Taschenbuch Verlag* and *Ullstein Bücher*.

E.C.M.
Newcastle upon Tyne, 1971

Acknowledgments

The author wishes to thank the following publishers for permission to quote from the works of Heinrich Böll of which they control the copyright:

Friedrich Middelhauve Verlag
Verlag Kiepenheuer und Witsch

Thanks are due also to Verlag Kiepenheuer und Witsch for permission to quote from *In Sachen Böll* edited by Marcel Reich-Raniki and *Der Schriftsteller Heinrich Böll* edited by Werner Lengning, and to the Athenäum Verlag GMBH for a passage from *Rhythmus und Figur* by Klaus Jeziorkowski.

Gratitude is expressed to Somerville College, Oxford, for affording leisure to carry out research and to Alixe Short for her patient typing of the manuscript, and to Dr. B. J. Kenworthy and Olive Sayce for their helpful suggestions.

Biographical Note

Heinrich Böll was born on 21 December 1917, the eighth child of Victor Böll, in Cologne. In his essay *Über mich selbst*, published in 1958, he describes his ancestry and his childhood years in the city. His paternal forbears were ships' carpenters, Catholics who emigrated from England during the reign of Henry VIII. From Holland, they moved up the Rhine, settled in Cologne and became joiners. His forbears on his mother's side were farmers and brewers. Böll's childhood memories are of his father's workshop, with its smells of glue, varnish and freshly planed wood, and of the blocks of flats behind it, crowded with people who sang, cursed and hung out their washing. The family lived near the Rhine. The river and the old streets of Cologne formed the setting for his early life. Böll is essentially 'of the people'. From his stock and his childhood environment derives that deep insight into the fears and aspirations of the ordinary man which gives to his work the stamp of authenticity.

To the formative influence of a working-class background was added the religious atmosphere of a Catholic home. Böll was born a Catholic and wishes to die in that faith, but refuses to become involved in dissensions between different factions in the Church. He states quite plainly (1963): 'Ich gehöre keiner Gruppe an' (*Aufsätze Kritiken Reden*, p. 457). In articles and essays, and in the novels, he attacks the inadequacies of the Church, its intellectual affectations and political infighting, but his catholic/religious background enables him to emerge from despair and disintegration through love and religion to an awareness of positive values and the essential dignity of man.

His earliest memory was of sitting on his mother's arm to see the return of Hindenburg's beaten army and hearing his father curse the war and 'that fool of an Emperor'. He grew up during the 1920s and 1930s in an atmosphere of industrial strikes, political demonstrations and inflation. With a note for one million marks he bought a stick of barley sugar. The stabilization of the mark brought with it unemployment and poverty, and school friends whose fathers were out of work would beg him for a piece of bread during school break. His own background reasonably secure, he remained at school until he had taken his Abitur, but the general climate of unrest and poverty left a lasting impression.

After a short period of training as an assistant in a bookshop, during which time he made some first attempts at creative writing, Böll was called to do military service in autumn, 1938. The following summer found him in the Army, where he served as an infantryman throughout the war on several fronts, from Cap Gris Nez to the Crimea, and was wounded three times. The last months of the war were spent in an American prisoner-of-war camp. Six years of war provided the material for two novels and countless short stories but, more important, they shaped his conception of the nature of existence and brought him face to face with despair.

After the war Böll returned to Cologne, became a student and worked part of the time in the joiner's workshop belonging to his brother. He began to write again. The war experience had given him the material and released his creative powers. From 1947 his short stories were accepted for publication in literary magazines and newspapers. He wrote radio plays and finally took the decision to make writing his profession. The following years more than justified the risks involved. Böll has become one of the most important and most successful writers to emerge from post-war Germany. His works have been translated into several languages both in the West and in Eastern Europe where he is equally popular. He has achieved

fame not only as a writer of popular stories but also as a writer
of literary standing, and has received the following awards in
recognition of his achievements:

- 1951   Preis der Gruppe 47
- 1952   René-Schickele-Preis
- 1953   Deutscher Kritikerpreis
- 1953   Literaturpreis des Bundesverbandes der deutschen
          Industrie
- 1955   Preis der 'Tribune de Paris'
- 1958   Staatspreis von Nordrhein-Westfalen
- 1959   Der große Kunstpreis von Nordrhein-Westfalen
- 1960   Charles-Veillon-Preis
- 1961   Literaturpreis der Stadt Köln
- 1966   Premio Calabria (Italien)
- 1967   Georg-Büchner-Preis

Today, he lives with his wife and children, mostly in Cologne.
He has travelled widely but in Southern Ireland he has discovered a largely unspoiled country in which he feels at home.
To Böll, Ireland is a refuge from the materialism of his own
country and of much of the Western world. The rich humanity
and simple devoutness of its people uniquely combined with
their natural gaiety and ready wit mirror the two poles of his
own nature: the lively humour and real compassion which find
such finely balanced expression in his work.

1

War: The Decisive Influence

Any attempt to understand and evaluate the stories and novels of Heinrich Böll must first take into account the traumatic experience fundamental to all his work, the war and its chaotic aftermath. This was the experience of a whole generation, but in the case of Böll is added the further misery of serving a régime he despised.

He was fifteen years old when the Nazi Party came to power in Germany and from the age of twenty-one to twenty-eight his was the rootless, homeless, often boring existence of an unwilling soldier. His life was spent in transit in a world where nothing was stable, nothing permanent.

1. Es ist zu viel vorgekommen, zu viel Leeres geredet, zu wenig getan worden in der Zeit, die uns ins verantwortliche Alter geführt hat . . . Wartesäle, Lager, Hospitäler, Schlangestehen um Brot, Zigaretten und zur Entlassung . . . (*Frankfurter Vorlesungen*, p. 84)

   Too much has happened, too many empty words have been spoken, too little done at the time when we attained the age of responsibility. Waiting rooms, camps, hospitals, queues for bread, for cigarettes and for demobilization . . .

And perhaps most important of all, although he had wanted the war to be lost, he had to witness the horrors of destruction and annihilation which came with total collapse. It is important to note that none of Böll's stories touch on the earlier triumphs of the German Army. These did not concern him. The war stories are set after 1943 and tell only of retreat and defeat. It was the pointless horror of this protracted period and the chaos of the immediate post-war years that concentrated and fused his feelings and gave the form in which to express them. It transformed him into Heinrich Böll, the mouthpiece of countless inarticulate helpless human beings emerging from the ruins of Europe.

2. Schreiben wollte ich immer, versuchte es schon früh, fand aber die Worte erst später. (*Hierzulande: Aufsätze zur Zeit*, p. 9)

I had always wanted to write, I tried it at an early age but not until later did I find the words.

A. Content

Böll's novels are concerned with the position of the individual within the framework of society. His pessimistic views on this uneasy relationship, crystallized and given expression by his experience of total defeat, are not modified as material conditions in Germany change for the better. Böll appears to live within a central revelation from which successive novels radiate, making it unrewarding to examine them chronologically in terms of progressive development other than from the point of view of style. The deep pessimism of *Entfernung von der Truppe* is quite as unrelieved as is the desperate hopelessness of the early short stories and *Irisches Tagebuch* offers as much a solution as *Ende einer Dienstfahrt*. Each work serves to illuminate a continuing state rather than a change or development in Böll's beliefs.

War was for Böll an experience of senseless horror and wanton wastefulness. He looks through the eyes of soldiers crouching in holes in the ground, fighting not only against the enemy but also against dirt, lice and hopelessness. Nowhere is there the slightest hint of glory, of nobility, of heroic

self-sacrifice. Without illusions, those involved see only the
other face of war.

> 1. Zu oft und zu innig hatten wir seine zähnefletschende
> Fratze gesehen, und sein grauenhafter Atem . . . hatte
> uns zu oft das Herz erzittern gemacht. Wir haßten ihn zu
> sehr, als daß wir noch glauben mochten an die Seifen-
> blasen der Phrasen, die das Gesindel hüben und drüben
> aufsteigen ließ, um ihm den Wert einer „Sendung" zu
> geben. (*Wanderer, kommst du nach Spa . . .* p. 97)

> We had seen its snarling face too often and at too close range and its
> horrid breath had made our hearts tremble too frequently. We hated
> it too much for us to be able to have faith in it or in the soap-bubble
> phrases which rise from the rubble on both sides, to give it the stature
> of a sacred mission.

Life is bereft of meaning because there is no permanency. The
future is a black tunnel, impenetrable and full of sharp corners;
the past has receded and become a dream; the present is a time
of fear.

> 2. . . . denn wir hatten Angst, alle, die noch menschlich
> waren, hatten Angst. (Ibid., p. 99)

> . . . for we were afraid, everyone who was still human was afraid.

Böll expresses this fear and despair in the image of the individual, essentially alone as an inimical world disintegrates
around him. It is the image of the old soldier in the short story
In der Finsternis:

> 3. . . . blaß und schmal und unrasiert und hatte ein
> Niemandsgesicht . . . [er] blies die Kerze aus und lag in
> völligem Dunkel ganz allein in der Erde. (Ibid., p. 104/111)

> pale and thin and unshaven with the face of a nobody he blew out
> the candle and lay in the earth, quite alone in complete darkness.

The individual without identity, in *complete darkness* and *quite alone*. This is the assessment of the human condition given in Böll's early work; the individual, isolated and of no importance, existing in an alien, disintegrating world is basic to Böll. Böll is agonizingly aware of the essential loneliness of each one in a world of unrelated phenomena, of things unrelated to him and to each other, itself with no inherent meaning or value. Its only reality is that bestowed upon it by the individual himself. This view of separate existence, although always present, finds its clearest and most poignant expression much later in the creation of the clown, Hans Schnier.

> 4. Hans Schnier macht Ernst mit der Entdeckung Kants, daß der vermeintlich objektive Raum und entsprechend die vermeintlich objektive Zeit und Kausaltität eben doch nur Anschauungsformen und Kategorien des Menschen sind, die nicht wahrhaftig objektiv in der Welt selbst angelegt sind. (Jeziorkowski, *Rhythmus und Figur*, p. 187)

> Kant's discovery, that ostensibly objective space and corresponding ostensibly objective time and causality are merely intuitive forms and categories of man, which have no actual objective validity in the world, is only too real to Hans Schnier.

Although society forces its pattern onto life, the individual is isolated in a world that not only makes no sense to him but is itself devoid of sense. It is an alien monster, anonymous and abstract. For the most part Böll presents the individual in the form of a simple man or woman, without money, position or influence, manipulated by some remote, uncomprehended power—a power that they externalize as the ever-recurring 'sie' of the stories—and it is tempting to see in Böll merely the champion of the 'little man' against an unjust society. But this view is superficial. At a deeper level Böll's 'kleiner Mensch' is a symbol for all humanity, vulnerable, without shelter and without protection, subject to the unwieldy, senseless world.

B. Form

(*a*) The influence of the disintegrating experience of war
spreads over from the theme of Böll's work into the fabric of
the style, giving that unity of content and form which makes the
novels so readable. His apprehension of the external world as
a fragmented, unrelated, motiveless collection of phenomena is
reflected in the 'realistic' style of his writing. A feature of this
style is the minute detail with which Böll builds up descriptive
passages. Telephone calls are made and each detail of the
kiosk, of the finding of the coin, of the turning of the dial and
the breathless waiting for a response is enumerated. The
description of the banknotes sent to Käte by Fred Bogner *Und
sagte kein einziges Wort* occupies sixteen lines. In the same
novel Fred escapes from the rain-drenched streets into a snack
bar. As he eats he gazes into a mirror and fails at first to
recognize his own reflection.

1. Und während ich jetzt die Wurst aß, deren Wärme an
meinem wunden Zahnfleisch heftige Schmerzen hervorrief
. . . sah ich die Gesichter meiner Nebenmänner im Spiegel,
Münder, die aufgerissen waren, um in die Würste zu
beißen, ich sah dunkle, gähnende Gaumen hinter gelben
Zähnen, in die rosiges Wurstfleisch brockenweise hinein-
fiel, sah gute Hüte, schlechte und die nassen Haare
hutloser Zeitgenossen, zwischen denen das rosige Gesicht
der Würstchenverkäuferin hin und her ging. Munter
lächelnd angelte sie heiße Würste mit der Holzgabel aus
schwimmendem Fett, kleckste Senf auf Pappe, ging hin
und her zwischen diesen essenden Mündern, sammelte
schmutzige, mit Senf bekleckerte Pappteller ein, gab
Zigaretten und Limonade aus, nahm Geld ein, Geld mit
ihren rosigen, etwas zu kurzen Fingern, während der
Regen auf das Zeltdach trommelte. (*Und sagte kein
einziges Wort*, p. 7)

And while I ate the sausages the heat of which made my sore gums hurt terribly, I saw the faces of people near me in the mirror, mouths opened wide to bite into sausages, I saw dark yawning gums behind yellow teeth into which pink sausage meat fell, piece by piece, I saw good hats, poor ones, and the wet hair of those of my contemporaries who had no hats, and the rosy face of the girl who sold the sausages, moving backwards and forwards. Smiling gaily, she fished the hot sausages from the swimming fat with a wooden fork, daubed mustard onto cardboard plates, walked up and down among those eating mouths collecting the dirty mustard-blotched plates, distributed cigarettes and lemonade, took money, money with her pink rather stunted fingers, and all the time the rain drummed on the canvas roof.

Here we have a scene reflected through a *mirror*. This is a device which, together with that of the *mask*, recurs frequently, for both have the capacity to distort and alienate. Added to this initial alienation we have a detailed description which ostensibly presents a coherent whole and yet, rather frighteningly, has precisely the opposite effect. This detail serves only to emphasize the enormity and incomprehensibility of what we see. The eating mouths have an existence of their own, divorced from their human framework. The drenched hair, the wooden fork, the swimming fat and the mustard-daubed paper plates, the pink sausages and the pink fingers of the pink-faced girl move in the depths of the mirror, banal, indifferent objects which register in isolation. Wolfdietrich Rasch who, together with Jeziorkowski, sees Böll's importance as a writer in the style rather than in the content of his work, sums up its peculiar effect. Of individual objects in a description he writes:

2. . . . erscheinen sie manchmal fast gespenstisch in ihrer Vereinzelung, als sinnleere, zusammenhanglose Fakten, isoliert und armselig. Diese Dinge sind nicht mehr Repräsentanten eines spürbaren Zusammenhanges, der sie bindet und trägt, nicht mehr Glieder einer sinnerfüllten Einheit, sondern Zeichen des Zerfalls solcher Einheitswelt, Zeichen der Fremdheit. Die tiefe Entfremdung zwischen

Mensch und Welt verdeutlicht sich im penetranten
Eigenleben dieser gehäuften Belanglosigkeiten und unver-
bundenen Einzelheiten, die unsere sichtbare Realität
weithin ausmachen. (Rasch: *Lobrede und Deutung* in *Der
Schriftsteller Heinrich Böll*, pp. 14–15)

> They appear almost spectral in their isolation, like senseless un-
> connected things, remote and paltry. These things are no longer
> representative of a detectable whole which connects and carries them
> along, no longer members of a meaningful unity but signs of the
> collapse of such a unified world, signs of alienation. The deep es-
> trangement between man and the world is underlined in the way
> these inconsequential things and unrelated details, enumerated at
> length, which make up our visible reality, seem to possess a life of
> their own.

Things appearing in isolation are devoid of sense, they lack
a binding force to make them part of a meaningful whole, they
are deformed, unrelated and without objective reality. Each
one must provide his own key, his own interpretation and the
more sensitive experience the agony of their awareness that
this is self-imposed and therefore has no objective validity.
Minute detail, *distortion* and *alienation* are key attributes of
Böll's style as he presents for us the chronic insecurity of man.
The mirror already mentioned in a previous quotation is a
recurring device to this end, adding to the horror of the individual who sees himself, yet a stranger, as no more valid than
other external objects, other people, multiplied around him.
Nauseated, the child Martin *Haus ohne Hüter* hurries through
the restaurant, hoping to escape before he is sick, and feels
himself lost in an eternity of people all eating:

3. . . . eine Unendlichkeit fressender Menschen . . . grund-
   zende Fresser, deren gerötete Gesichter er doppelt sah in
   den Spiegeln. (*Haus ohne Hüter*, p. 106)

   > . . . grunting eaters whose flushed faces he saw multiplied in the
   > mirrors.

Käte Bogner *Und sagte kein einziges Wort* catches sight of herself involuntarily, and beyond the remote white face she becomes absorbed in time past. It is a struggle to return to the reality of the present, to her own dead, disinterested reflection.

4. Es gelingt mir nicht, meinen Blick aus dem Spiegel zurückzuholen, ihn auf mein Gesicht zu lenken, von dem ich weiß, daß es nicht lächelte. (*Und sagte kein einziges Wort*, p. 40)

> I am unable to drag back my eyes from the depths of the mirror, to focus them on my face which I know is not smiling.

Hans Schnier *Ansichten eines Clowns* carries out his facial exercises before the mirror into which he stares until he ceases to exist:

5. . . . bis ich zuletzt gar nicht mehr da war: . . . Ich vergaß einfach, daß ich es war, dessen Gesicht ich da im Spiegel sah, . . . das war ein fremder Kerl in meinem Badezimmer . . . ich habe Angst, verrückt zu werden. (*Ansichten eines Clowns*, p. 146)

> . . . I simply forgot that it was I whose face I saw there in the mirror . . . that was a stranger in my bathroom . . . I'm frightened I shall go mad.

When he is alone, he is obsessed by the fear that there will be no one around to bring him back from the depths of the mirror where he reels and tumbles as on slippery ice.

A closely related image to that of the mirror is that of the *mask*, and once more it is in Schnier that the image finds its greatest realization. Schnier is a clown and must appear to his public in one of his many masks, and this way of life completes his alienation from himself and from others. It is a form of suicide because he himself is no longer sure which is the real Schnier, *meine wahre Meinung, mein wahres Gesicht, mein wahres Ich*, my genuine opinion, my real face, my true identity. He makes himself up before the mirror, painting his face an unrelieved white, unable to distinguish what is real, what is part of the act.

6. Es war das Gesicht eines Selbstmörders, und als ich anfing, mich zu schminken, war mein Gesicht das Gesicht eines Toten . . . ich dachte keinen Augenblick daran, daß ich selbst es war, den ich sah. Das war kein Clown mehr, ein Toter, der einen Toten spielte. (*Ansichten eines Clowns*, pp. 230–1)

It was the face of a suicide and when I began to put on my make-up, my face was the face of a dead man . . . I did not think for a moment that it was myself I saw. It was not a clown any more, it was a dead man playing the part of a dead man.

But the mask is not only the professional guise of the clown. It has become standard equipment for modern living. In the faceless society of today it has become necessary for the individual to become faceless and indistinguishable, to follow the rules and wear the inoffensive mask of conformity. In the grim short story *Mein trauriges Gesicht* the narrator is sentenced to ten years imprisonment for having a sad face when the State had decreed that such an expression was illegal.

7. Ich aber muß versuchen, gar kein Gesicht mehr zu haben . . . (*Wanderer, kommst du nach Spa . . .* p. 149)

As for me, I must try not to have any face at all . . .

Der Wegwerfer, the man who earns his living by throwing away unnecessary circulars and brochures arriving in the post, delights secretly in the knowledge that he does not conform to society but takes care not to give rise to suspicion:

8. Ich biete den Anblick eines Bürgers. (*Nicht nur zur Weihnachtszeit*, p. 123)

9. So vollende ich das Bild eines gepflegten Mitbürgers . . . Das Air der Rechtschaffenheit umgibt mich wie der gläserne Sarg Schneewitchen umgab. (Ibid., p. 124)

I present the appearance of an ordinary citizen.

In this way I perfect the image of a well-groomed member of society . . . The air of righteousness encloses as like the glass coffin enclosed Snowwhite.

He plays the part of a well-behaved, trusted member of society, and whenever he catches sight of his face reflected in the window of his morning tram, he schools it into the prescribed shape:

10. [ich] versuche, meinem Gesicht den Ausdruck zu geben, den es haben soll . . . (Ibid., p. 125)

I try to give my face the expression which it ought to wear . . .

Böll's writing is rich in imagery and symbolism. The train, the station, the lifeless manipulated puppet, emphasize the essential insecurity, transitoriness and powerlessness of the individual, but the mask and mirror exemplify most clearly the unease of Böll face to face with individual existence. The basic experience of Böll, '*die Entfremdung zwischen Mensch und Welt*',[1] is reflected in the *realism of his style* and the *imagery* he chooses.

(*b*) The style of writing illustrates and emphasizes the theme and it is further reinforced by the form of presentation which emerges with the novels, primitively in *Der Zug war pünktlich*, but subsequently becoming basic and finding its most successful expression in *Billard um halb zehn*. Just as the world in which

[1] cf. pp. 9–10, Quote 2.

we exist is not as it seems, a cogent comprehensible whole, interrelated and universally valid, so time is also shown to be different from how we apprehend it, that is as past, present and future.

Since the catastrophe of the war Böll felt that the past was dead and the gulf between contemporary divided Germany and pre-Nazi Germany unbridgeable, making past traditions and way of life invalid. Yet the past cannot be ignored, glossed over and forgotten, and as a writer he is concerned that in some way past and present should be integrated to form a solid basis for the future. Hence the technique of Böll's novels with their peculiar use of time. In his perceptive article 'Time in the works of Heinrich Böll' James Reid discusses the montage technique of Böll which enables him, while setting his novels in the present, to portray the past in a series of flashbacks and reminiscences. Böll does not present a straightforward linear narrative, for to him time is not an ordered progression. Nothing is fixed and stable. Time is cut into sections connected in non-chronological order and is not time as we know it. In his radio play *Klopfzeichen* Böll writes:

11. Man kann in die Zeit fallen, wie in ein Loch; da ist alles gegenwärtig, vergangen, zukünftig—und du weißt nicht, ob das Vergangene Gegenwart oder das Gegenwärtige Zukunft ist. Es ist eins. (*Zum Tee bei Dr. Borsig*, p. 153)

One can fall into time as into a hole; there everything is present, past and future and you don't know whether the past is the present or the present is the future. It is all one.

The individual lives in a kind of eternity; time is relative, even a plaything in the hands of Heinrich Fähmel *Billard um halb zehn* as, on his eightieth birthday, he looks back upon the deliberate game—once more an alienating action—he has played with his life in lonely isolation.

12. . . . noch schwamm ich auf der Zeit dahin, versank in
    Wellentälern, überquerte die Ozeane Vergangenheit und
    Gegenwart und drang, durch Einsamkeit vorm Versinken
    gesichert, tief in die eisige Kälte der Zukunft, hatte als
    eiserne Ration mein Lachen mit, von dem ich nur sparsam
    kostete . . . (*Billard um halb zehn*, p. 91)

> . . . I was still swimming along on time. I sank down in the troughs
> between the waves, crossed the oceans of past and present and, secure
> against drowning by my loneliness, I pressed on into the icy coldness
> of the future, carrying with me as iron rations my laughter which I
> only used sparingly . . .

Similarly his wife, Johanna, living in physical isolation in the
asylum, although not insane and not unaware of the actual
date on the calendar, chooses to live in the past. She expresses
herself in similar imagery:

13. . . . verschone mich mit dem Kalender in deinen Augen;
    ich fahre dahin auf dem winzigen Kalenderblatt, das den
    Namen 31. Mai 1942 trägt; zerstöre nicht das Papier-
    schiffchen, aus einem Kalenderblatt gefaltet, und stürz
    mich nicht in den Ozean der sechzehn Jahre. (Ibid., p. 123)

> . . . spare me the calendar in your eyes, I travel along on the tiny page
> from the calendar which bears the name 31 May 1942; don't destroy
> the little paper ship, folded from the calendar page, and don't plunge
> me into the ocean of these sixteen years.

To sum up: neither in the world of things nor that of time is
there a fixed and stable point of reference. This is the philosophy
basic to Böll and reflected in the fabric of his writing. This is
the legacy of total defeat experienced by his generation in
Germany combined with the disillusion and bitterness of the
post-war world. For this Böll found the words. This is not to
say that Böll is a negative writer, nothing more than the carping
critic he is sometimes held to be. Nor are his stories and novels

unrelievedly gloomy since his awareness of the absurdity of man's position gives him a keen eye for the ludicrous, comical and grotesque situations which find hilarious expression in the satires. It is his very awareness of the fundamental problem of existence which forces him to denounce contemporary life as he seeks a constructive approach to some deeper reality by which contemporary man might survive.

2

Böll's Critical Writings

The basic problem of human existence for Böll is *isolation*. As we have seen the individual is totally alone, unsure of his identity in a hostile world, and unable to communicate at the deepest level. Böll's aim therefore is to find some means to enable him to survive *within the framework of society*. Only through *contact with his fellow-man* is there hope of alleviating his loneliness and giving some purpose to his life. Society is examined and found wanting. What Böll finds, gives little hope. The structure of society in the Federal Republic, as in most Western countries, is geared to wealth, business, material gain, trade expansion and all the outer trappings of a successful economy. It offers as little protection to the individual as he would find in the jungle and as little chance of survival. Society is an economic jungle where wild beasts lurk (*eine Wirtschafts-dschungel, wo die Bestien lauern*). In such a society, which puts a premium on the survival of the fittest, the innocent, the sick, the weak, the crippled are completely defenceless. As a Catholic, Böll sees that the only hope for these dispossessed ones lies within the framework of a Christian rather than a non-Christian society, and looks to the priests and the bishops for a lead. Here too he feels his search is in vain. These shepherds are silent. He finds so little evidence of practical Christianity in contemporary West Germany he can only marvel

> . . . daß sich diese westliche Welt noch als christlich deklariert. (*Frankfurter Vorlesungen*, p. 112)

> . . . that this Western world still declares itself to be Christian.

Since the Church does not give the moral lead Böll looks to the writer to expose the injustices of society.

A. The Writer: Basic Concerns

(*a*) COMMITMENT

In the *Frankfurter Vorlesungen* given in May 1964 Heinrich Böll speaks of his own attitude as a writer.

> 1. Obwohl als einzelner schreibend, ausgestattet nur mit einem Stoß Papier, einem Kasten gespitzter Bleistifte einer Schreibmaschine, habe ich mich nie als einzelnen empfunden, sondern als Gebundenen. Gebunden an Zeit und Zeitgenossenschaft, an das von einer Generation Erlebte, Erfahrene, Gesehene und Gehörte . . . (*Frankfurter Vorlesungen*, p. 7)

> Although writing as an individual, equipped with a pile of paper, a box of sharpened pencils, a typewriter, I have never felt myself an isolated but a committed writer, committed to my time and to my contemporaries, to all that is experienced, learned, seen and heard by my generation . . .

Like thousands of others he has lived through the war and through its aftermath. His experiences have been the same as theirs. He is as much a product of his time as they are and as responsible for its insufficiencies. Literature, then, for him is not an ivory tower interested only in aesthetic matters. The first concern of the writer is that he should be *involved* with his time, with the problems and lives of his fellow-men. In March 1970, speaking at the 'Woche der Brüderlickeit' in Cologne, Böll reaffirms these beliefs.

> 2. Mein Autor lebt nicht auf einem Leuchtturm, der Reinheit ausstrahlt, rings um Schmutz entdeckt, und nun im Vollglanz seiner Reinheit diesen Schmutz zu beschimpfen

beginnt. Mein Autor lebt auf der Erde, aus der er gemacht wird und seine Bitterkeit ist die Bitterkeit der Erde, aus der er gemacht ist. Er ist Brotesser, Biertrinker, Steuerzahler, Kinogänger u.s.w. (*Anspruch zur Eröffnung der Woche der Brüderlichkeit* 1970 im Kölner Gürzenich. Kölner Stadt Anzeiger, 9 March 1970)

My author does not live in a lighthouse discovering squalor all around in the beams of purity which stream from it and in the full illumination of its purity begins to curse this squalor. My author lives on the earth from which he is made, and his bitterness is the bitterness of the earth from which he is made. He eats bread, drinks beer, pays taxes, goes to the cinema, etc.

The writer, then, is not a being apart. He is as other men, experiencing their sorrows, their joys and their desires, living as they live, the product of a common experience. But in one thing he is different. He is articulate and his gift enables him to do more than suffer and experience with them. He can *express* their despair. He goes on to say:

3. Was ihn von den Erdbewohnern um ihn herum ein wenig abheben mag, ist vielleicht die Fähigkeit, sich auszudrücken, auch die Fähigkeit öffentlich auszusprechen, was als unaussprechbar gilt. (Ibid.)

What may well elevate him a little from others is perhaps the ability to express himself and also the ability to express in public what is considered to be unmentionable.

He has not only the ability to express himself, to be articulate, but also the duty to express publicly what might otherwise be suppressed. There is a need to cry out, to reveal what is rotten beneath the surface. There is a need to express the horror of the war. Such an obscenity must not be glossed over in a frenzy of heroism and patriotism. The strident cry must ring out, for in expression is the beginning of recognition and reconciliation.

It is a time for '*Aufschrei*' not '*humane Gelassenheit*'. It is not a
time to go gently. In his essay on *Wolfgang Borchert* (1955)
he says:

4. Es ist viel vom ,,Aufschrei Wolfgang Borcherts" geschrie-
ben und gesagt worden, und die Bezeichnung ,,*Aufschrei*"
wurde mit *Gelassenheit*[1] geprägt. Gelassene Menschen
ihrerseits schreien nicht— . . . Aber Kinder schreien, und
es tönt in die Gelassenheit der Weltgeschichte hinein der
Todesschrei Jesu Christi— (*Hierzulande*, p. 138)

   Much has been written and said about the scream of protest of
   Wolfgang Borchert, and the word 'scream' was chosen with cool
   composure. Cool composed people do not scream . . . but children
   scream and the dying scream of Jesus Christ rings out through the
   cool composure of the history of the world.

5. In der Memoirenliteratur begegnet uns so oft die humane
Gelassenheit, das müde Achselzucken des Pilatus, der
seine Hände in Unschuld wäscht. (Ibid. p. 137)

   In the War Memoirs we often come across humane composure, the
   weary shrug of the shoulder like Pilate who washed his hands in
   innocence.

The first concern, then, for the writer is *involvement*. It must
be the foundation on which his creativity is based. And in this
he must not compromise or make concessions. He cannot shrug
his shoulders and wash his hands.

6. Für mich ist das Engagement die Voraussetzung, es ist
sozusagen die Grundierung, und was ich auf dieser
Grundierung anstelle, ist das, was ich unter Kunst ver-
stehe. (Horst Bienek: *Werkstattgespräche mit Schrift-
stellern*, p. 49)

[1] Author's italics.

For me involvement is an initial assumption. It is, so to speak, the foundation, and what I construct on this foundation is what I understand by art.

(b) INTEGRITY

The writer must not only be involved and committed but his *integrity* must be beyond question. There must be no half-truths, no smooth words, no playing with meanings. A writer may well, with experience, acquire a different point of view but must never knowingly disseminate what he suspects to be lies. Mistakes may be made, but never with the intention to deceive.

7. Er kann irren, aber in dem Augenblick, wo er, was sich später als Irrtum herausstellen mag, ausspricht, muß er glauben, daß es die reine Wahrheit ist. (*Hierzulande*, pp. 113–14)

    He can be mistaken, but at the time he says what may well later turn out to be false, he must believe that it is the absolute truth.

The memory of the totalitarian State and Goebbels' Propaganda Ministry, of the spellbinding of Hitler, is still fresh enough in Böll's mind in 1955, and he is concerned that such dangers should not be forgotten. In the mouths of the Nazis language itself has been defiled.

8. Sie hat das Denken verseucht, die Luft, die wir atmen, sie hat die Worte, die wir sprechen und schreiben . . . vergiftet . . . (*Aufsätze Kritiken Reden*, p. 115)

    It [the national socialist sickness] has polluted thought, the air we breathe. It has poisoned the words we speak and write . . .

The search for a new language is a primary function of the post-war writer. The power of the written word is incalculable and it is a question of conscience whether the writer employs words to bring a new awareness or to defile and destroy. It is in the word *Gewissen* (conscience) that the key to Böll's approach lies.

> 9. . . . es werden nie mörderische Irrtümer und Torheiten sein, solange Sprache und Gewissen sich noch nicht getrennt haben . . . (*Hierzulande*, p. 113)

> . . . fatal mistakes will not be made, follies will not be committed as long as speech and conscience are inseparable . . .

As long as conscience and speech remain linked, the integrity of the writer will remain intact, but he can never afford to relax his vigilance in the service of truth.

(*c*) FREEDOM

If the writer is concerned for truth it follows that he must be concerned for his *freedom* to express that truth. As the voice of the inarticulate he must have absolute independence. As the servant of humanity he must never pay lip service to the State nor to any section of society with vested interests. Like any other citizen the writer pays his taxes but that must remain his only contact with the State. To put oneself in the service of any authority or régime, *die Herrschaften, die Mächtigen, sie*, is the worst crime an author can commit.

> 10. Der Schriftsteller, der sich dem Mächtigen beugt, sich gar ihm anbietet, wird auf eine fürchterliche Weise kriminell, er begeht mehr als Diebstahl, mehr als Mord. (*Hierzulande*, p. 113)

> The writer who bows to those in authority and is even prepared to offer himself to their service becomes a criminal in a particularly terrible way, he commits more than theft, more even than murder.

These are the three requirements for the post-war writer. He must be *involved* and *committed* but on the basis of *complete freedom* and *personal integrity*, or involvement counts for nothing.

B. The Approach to Reality

(*a*) REALITY AND ACTUALITY

Engagement has in the works of Heinrich Böll, however, a deeper meaning. Just as his literary work is layered, revealing to the perceptive student shades of meaning often unsuspected at first reading, so engagement is not merely an involvement in comparatively superficial, that is, social or political issues. In Böll's eyes the writer must not only speak for the inarticulate but also see for the shortsighted whose vision is bounded by the phenomena around them. He must see through the actual world into the real world, he must see the whole man in his setting. In his essay on Borchert, Böll differentiates between 'reporting' and 'creative writing'. Involvement and integrity are essential but in themselves not sufficient to mark off the writer from the journalist. *Insight* and *deeper vision* are the special qualities of the writer which enable him to become involved with human existence at its deepest level.

1. . . . der Anlaß der Reportage ist immer ein aktueller, eine Hungersnot, eine Überschwemmung, ein Streik—so wie der Anlaß einer Röntgenaufnahme immer ein aktueller ist: ein gebrochenes Bein, eine ausgerenkte Schulter. Das Röntgenfoto aber zeigt nicht nur die Stelle, wo das Bein gebrochen, wo die Schulter ausgerenkt war, es zeigt immer *zugleich* die Lichtpause des Todes, es zeigt den fotografierten Menschen in seinem Gebein, großartig und erschreckend. Wo das Röntgenauge eines Dichters durch das Aktuelle dringt, sieht es den ganzen Menschen, großartig und erschreckend . . . (*Hierzulande*, p. 139)

> ... the occasion of reporting is always an actual one, a famine, a flood, a strike—just as the occasion for an X-ray is an actual one, a broken leg, a dislocated shoulder. But the X-ray plate shows not only the place where the leg is broken, where the shoulder is dislocated, it shows at the same time the negative of death, it shows the X-rayed man as a skeleton, magnificent and intimidating. Where the X-ray eye of an imaginative writer penetrates, it sees the whole man, great and terrifying ...

With one's eyes one sees the *actual* world, *die Aktualität*; with the X-ray eyes of the writer one penetrates to the *real* world, *die Wirklichkeit*: the complete picture which makes sense of the often unrelated events comes into focus, and this is the world it is the duty of the writer to reveal. In this way he helps others to penetrate beyond externalities that delude by appearance.

2. ... wer Augen hat, zu sehen, für den werden die Dinge durchsichtig— (Ibid., p. 133)

> ... for him who has eyes to see, things become transparent.

3. ... ein gutes Auge gehört zum Handwerkszeug des Schriftstellers, ein Auge, gut genug, ihn auch Dinge sehen zu lassen, die in seinem optischen Bereich noch nicht aufgetaucht sind. (Ibid., p. 131)

> ... a good eye belongs among the tools of the writer, an eye good enough to see things which have not yet appeared in the range of his optical vision.

To see things not yet revealed to the normal field of vision one must turn within to the imagination.

4. Auch unsere Phantasie ist wirklich ... um aus den Tatsachen die Wirklichkeit zu entziffern. (Ibid., p. 63)

> Our imagination is real ... to enable us to decipher reality from the facts.

5. Aus dem Aktuellen das Wirkliche zu erkennen, dazu müssen wir unsere Vorstellungskraft in Bewegung setzen, eine Kraft, die uns befähigt, uns ein Bild zu machen. Das Aktuelle ist der Schlüssel zum Wirklichen. (Ibid., p. 65)

To recognize the real in the actual we must set our imagination to work, a faculty which enables us to form a picture. The actual is the key to the real.

The imagination, the inner vision, can evaluate phenomena and events happening in time and draw from them their essential, eternal meaning. It can form an image. This necessitates an *active participation* in our time and not a passive acceptance. Things are not explicit. Each one of us must try to evaluate what we see, but the writer, with his clearer vision, must be the guide. The keys are there for us. By means of our imagination we have only to recognize and use them to open up new vistas, new meanings. From these jigsaw pieces we can construct the complete picture.

6. Die Wirklichkeit wird uns nie geschenkt, sie erfordert unsere aktive, nicht unsere passive Aufmerksamkeit. Geliefert werden uns Schlüssel, Ziffern, ein Code—es gibt keinen Passepartout für die Wirklichkeit: Bücher, Tatsachen, sie sind immer nur . . . Teile von oder Schlüssel zu Wirklichkeiten, sie öffnen Wirklichkeiten wie man Türen zu Gebäuden öffnet, damit der Eintretende sich darin umsehe. (Ibid., p. 64)

Reality is never given to us, it demands our active, not passive attention. Keys are given to us, cyphers, a code—there is no framework for reality; books, facts, they are always only . . . parts of, or keys to, reality, they open up realities as one opens doors to buildings so that people may go in and look around.

Reality lies that little farther away from actuality and we must enter in and look round for it. Böll likens it to a letter addressed to each one of us; to a message which is given to us as a riddle to be solved; to a bird flying swiftly ahead. We must open the letter, we must try to solve the riddle, to shoot down the bird by firing ahead of it. We must draw conclusions: we must take the imaginative leap forward. This is necessary to our survival. Children are content with the actual. They live intensely in the moment, looking neither forward nor backward, in a moment which will never end in joy or in pain. They experience directly the grass, the wind, the water, the ball, the garishly coloured sugar stick, the eternity of the brightly coloured balloon. This Böll calls *die Wirklichkeit des Vergänglichen*—the reality of the transient—to which we too may surrender ourselves, unwisely, in the adult knowledge that these things are not permanent, that we are merely playing truant from school, that it is bound to come out and that we will be caught. For the balloon will burst, the sugar stick will melt, we cannot play truant from life. We can postpone things, but not indefinitely, and we are fully aware of this.

> 7. . . . aber wir wissen ja, wissen es leider, daß es kein permanentes Schulschwänzen gibt: daß wir den Vogel abschießen müssen, unser Leben nur in der Wirklichkeit vollziehen können: es geht auf Leben und Tod. (Ibid., p. 67)

> . . . but unfortunately we know only too well that there is no permanent truancy from school, that we shall have to shoot down the bird, that we can only fulfil our lives in reality; it is a matter of life and death.

Wir können unser Leben nur in der Wirklichkeit vollziehen: es geht auf Leben und Tod. This is Böll's fundamental conception. If we live like children in the present, perishable moment, if we limit our existence to the minute hand of the clock which divides the past from the future, then we are destroyed as each time-imprisoned moment is destroyed in the remorseless, perpetual

movement of time itself. The individual who accepts the actual
for the real is incapable of experiencing reality itself.

8. Wer den fliegenden Vogel treffen will, muß ruhig zielen,
   gelassen muß er auf dem Sekundenzeiger sitzen, der das
   Vergangene vom Zukünftigen trennt, und muß mutig in
   den luftleeren Raum schießen, auf daß der Vogel ins
   Geschoß hineinfliege und das Wirkliche ihm in die Hand
   falle. (Ibid., p. 66)

   He who wants to shoot the bird must take aim quietly, must sit calmly
   on the minute hand of the clock which divides the past from the
   future and must fire boldly into the airless void so that the bird flies
   into the bullet and reality falls into his hand.

Life, if it is to have any meaning at all, must be lived on a
higher, more imaginative level than that limited to day-to-day
existence. We must sit quietly and through our imagination
become aware of the existence of this higher reality, and only
when we live in this awareness do we live our lives to the full,
do we live at all.

9. Freilich gibt es Menschen, die ihr Leben routiniert leben;
   nur: sie leben nicht mehr. (Ibid., p. 153)

   Indeed there are people who have made a routine of their lives, but
   they are not living any more.

The 'engaged' writer involved at the deepest level in human
life has this task of unique importance: *to help us to distinguish
between life and death and to choose wisely*.

10. Kunst ist eine der wenigen Möglichkeiten, Leben zu
    haben und Leben zu halten, für den, der sie macht und für
    den, der sie empfängt. (Ibid., p. 152)

    Art is one of the few possibilities to have life and to keep it, for him
    who creates and for him who receives.

C. Trümmerliteratur. The Identification with Contemporary Events

Böll then sees it as the task of the writer, his own task, to reveal reality by looking at the world as it presents itself to his senses. *The contemporary scene is all important,* and he must concentrate on *die Tatsachen, das Aktuelle* which are the code by which he must decipher, the only code available. He must take what is given to him, the *environment in which he finds himself.* This Böll did. When he began to write, he wrote of his experiences as a serving soldier, and then as a demobilized soldier returning home. These were his 'facts' and he expressed them. Writers identified themselves with the men, women and children who lived in ruins and had emerged from a war they thought would never end, and wrote of what they themselves had experienced. In his essay *Bekenntnis zur Trümmerliteratur* Böll justifies this approach.

1. Wir schrieben also vom Krieg, von der Heimkehr und dem, was wir im Krieg gesehen hatten und bei der Heimkehr vorfanden: von Trümmern . . . es war Krieg gewesen, sechs Jahre lang, wir kehrten heim aus diesem Krieg, wir fanden Trümmer und schrieben darüber. (*Hierzulande*, pp. 128–9)

   So we wrote about the war, about coming home, and about what we had seen in the war, and had found as returning civilians: about ruins . . . there had been a war, war for six years. We came home from this war, we found ruins and wrote about them.

This method of writing, of recording the contemporary scene, is sometimes seen as one of Böll's limitations as a writer of stature, but to hold this view is to ignore Böll's whole conception of reality. There had been a war, the survivors were surrounded by ruined buildings, ruined lives, and not to write about them would have been to escape into a world of *Phantasterei.* He is careful to differentiate between this and *Phantasie.*

2. Phantasie hat nichts mit Phantasterei zu tun, nichts mit Phantomen—Phantasie, das ist unsere Vorstellungskraft, unsere Fähigkeit, uns ein Bild von etwas zu machen. (Ibid., p. 63)

Fantasy has nothing to do with fabrication, nothing to do with phantoms . . . Fantasy is our imagination, our ability to make an image of something.

To fabricate a fantastic world would be deliberately to ignore the code, to deceive, to miss the chance of getting to grips with reality.

3. Die Zeitgenossen in die Idylle zu entführen würde uns allzu grausam erscheinen, das Erwachen daraus wäre schrecklich, oder sollen wir Blindekuh miteinander spielen? (Ibid., p. 129)

To lure our contemporaries into an idyllic world seemed much too cruel to us, wakening up from it would be terrible, or should we be playing blind man's buff with one another?

In 1945 to write an idyll would have been meaningless and dangerous. Böll speaks of the suddenness with which the French Revolution burst upon the French nobility, like a thunderstorm from a clear sky. Lulled by almost a century of 'seclusion', dressed as shepherds and shepherdesses, playing and singing in artificially created 'natural' settings, they did not even begin to suspect the true state of affairs. They were accepting the false situation as the real one, in effect living a game of blind man's buff. They were *unaware*. Böll quotes Dickens as the example of an author with enough sense of humour to play blind man's buff from time to time, but, and this is the point:

4. . . . er hatte auch keine Binde vor den Augen . . . er lebte nicht im Blindekuhstand. (Ibid., pp. 130–1)

. . . he did not have a scarf tied over his eyes . . . he did not live in a state of blindness.

We are reminded of Böll's demand that the writer must write only what he knows to be true, that is of intrinsic value. Any other approach is to put on the blindfold and accept *Blindekuh nicht als Spiel, sondern als Zustand* (ibid., p. 131), blind man's buff not as a game but as a way of life.

Homer, too, wrote *Trümmerliteratur*. He wrote of the Trojan War, the sacking of Troy, the return of Odysseus: *Kriegs-Trümmer- und Heimkehrerliteratur*. The important thing is that the writer should mirror what he sees so that the lesson of reality may be learned. Böll's criticism of West Germany, and indirectly of Western Europe, is that the lesson has not been learned. We have not understood how to live our lives as we should, have not mastered a basic skill, that of living our lives only in reality.

D. Böll: Social Critic

(*a*) LOST OPPORTUNITIES

The early stories and novels of Böll can be classified as *Trümmerliteratur*. Initially born of the suffering and chaos of war they are concerned with shattered cities, retreating armies and the dazed emergence from the ruins of a former way of life. The tangible enemy is gone, the old order has disappeared. It is a chaotic, desperate time and yet, contrarily, a time of hope, a chance to start again and take a fresh look at society, a time of *revaluation* and *opportunity*. As horrific as the war and the Nazi period have been, the following years are to reveal a deeper despair. It is to be a tragic time of lost opportunities, bringing the full realization that nothing has changed. This is the burden of Böll's later work.

In the novels we can relive the German experience since the war. Progress has been made, the economic miracle has come to pass, but it has been progress on a material plain only. There are more and more sugar sticks, endless bright balloons to dazzle and delude, but the hopes of a just, humane society have foundered in a morass of materialism. The farther the economic miracle progresses, the clearer it becomes that nothing fundamental has been changed. Society is still unjust, there is no equality, no lesson has been learned. The Establishment is still the Establishment standing as firmly as ever on the triple pillars of State, Army and Church. These three, a formidable Trinity of vested interest, comprise the framework of society—a framework from which Böll in 1970 wishes to escape as much as he had done twenty or even thirty years previously. In his address to those assembled to celebrate the yearly *Woche der Brüderlichkeit*, held in Cologne in March 1970, he says:

1. . . . erlaube mir nur, mich im Jahre 1970 ausdrücklich, nachdrücklich und endgültig aus einem Rahmen zu entfernen, der in der Anwesenheit der überkommenen Trinität Staat, Kirche, Armee eine Woche der Brüderlichkeit eröffnet. (*Kolner Stadt-Anzeiger*, 9 March 1970)

. . . just permit me in the year 1970, expressly, emphatically and finally to withdraw from the set-up which, in the presence of the traditional Trinity of State, Church and Army inaugurates a Week of Brotherliness.

(*b*) BÖLL'S BUNDESREPUBLIK

Böll wishes to withdraw from a society which is hypocritical enough to hold a week of brotherly love while still rejecting all who do not conform to the accepted social code: *die Gammler, die Lang-haarigen, die Schmutzfinken, die Obdachlosen, die Asozialen*—the drop-outs, the long-haired, the layabouts, the homeless, the anti-social. A society in which a young couple in search of housing accommodation encounters the outer limits of brotherhood fixed beyond their income should not be indulging in such a charade. The word *Brüderlichkeit* is bereft of meaning.

1. The Indictment
Bitterly disappointed that the opportunity to make a new start
has slipped away, Böll never ceases to attack a state which has
been preoccupied exclusively with a programme of national
development and economic recovery so that it might regain its
self-esteem and become a nation of consequence. In the
Federal Republic itself Böll sees yet another manifestation of
the actual and the real. To all intents and purposes it is a fact,
an actual new state, but in reality it is only a fabricated thing;
divided Germany is no longer a real country. It is a country so
imprecise that it is difficult to form a real conception of it.
It defies analysis.

1. Für dieses gemischte Gebilde, das Bundesrepublik heißt,
   eine Formel zu finden, dazu wäre sogar ein Einstein der
   Formulierung nicht fähig. (*Hierzulande*, p. 10)

   Even an Einstein would not be capable of finding a definition for this
   confused structure that is called the Federal Republic.

This new Germany is not *bewohnbar*, a land to be lived in, and
its nationals, the West Germans, are *Überlebende, die Wohnung
suchen*, survivors seeking a home. Hence Böll's insistence that
the first task of the new writers should be the search for a
humane, mutually comprehensible language in a country which
can be lived in. In the same lecture, Böll goes on to define such
a country:

2. Ein Land ist bewohnt und bewohnbar, wenn einer Heimweh nach ihm empfinden kann. (*Frankfurter Vorlesungen*,
   p. 57)

   A country can be said to be really inhabited and habitable if one can
   feel homesick for it.

There may be many who feel this homesickness, but it is only for a Germany that no longer exists and for which the Federal Republic is a poor, if not ridiculous substitute.

3. Heimweh nach der Bundesrepublik? Vielleicht gibt es das. Ob dieses Land so werden kann, daß man nach ihm Heimweh empfinden könnte? (Ibid., p. 58)

Homesickness for the Federal Republic? Perhaps there is such a thing. But is it possible that it could become the kind of country that one could feel homesick for?

West Germany, under Böll's scrutiny, falls lamentably short of the hoped-for, post-war dream.

State, Church and Army, the Establishment, the Manipulators—all are dominated by political considerations. Politics and political ethics pervade the whole of life, and actions in every sphere are politically motivated.

4. Wir werden gezwungen, von Politik zu leben—und das ist eine fragwürdige Kost, da gibt es, je nach den Erfordernissen der Taktik, an einem Tag Pralinen, am anderen eine Suppe aus Dörrgemüse. (*Hierzulande*, p. 45)

We are compelled to nourish ourselves on politics—and that is very questionable fare, according to the demands of tactics, one day we have sweets, the next dried vegetable soup.

5. es gibt ja keine religiösen Auseinandersetzungen mehr, nur noch politische, und selbst religiöse Entscheidungen, wie die des Gewissens, werden zu politschen gestempelt: magere Jahre stehen bevor . . . (Ibid., p. 44)

No longer do we have religious confrontations and discussions, only political ones, and even religious decisions, like those of conscience, bear the stamp of politics: lean years lie ahead . . .

In the political game one must be alert, swift and agile enough to be in the right place at the right time. Politics is in the hands of the tacticians to whom political victories alone are important. Society has for Böll become the *Catchergesellschaft*, the opportunist society.

> 6. . . . die Catcher beherrschen das Feld, die Primitiv-Taktiker, Männer ohne Erinnerungsvermögen, die Vitalen, Gesunden, die nicht „rückwärts blicken" . . . (Ibid., p. 44)

> . . . the 'wide boys' carry the day; the unscrupulous tacticians, men unable to remember, those full of strength and health who never look back . . .

With the reform of currency and the return of prosperity society is corrupted. Satiated with things, it seeks the shadow rather than the substance, assesses a man by his status symbols, not by what he is. Appearance carries more weight than essence.

> 7. Für eine übersättigte Welt ist die Nußschale wichtiger als der Kern; den wirft man weg, kratzt aus der Schale alles heraus, das an einen Inhalt, einen Zweck erinnern könnte, poliert die Schale, . . . denn sie ist so schön . . . (Ibid., p. 58)

> In a world which has too much, the shell is more important than the kernel; that is thrown away; everything is scraped out of the shell which could possibly hint at content or purpose, the shell is polished . . . for it looks so lovely . . .

This is Böll's indictment of German society. It is greedy and undiscerning; it accepts everything at face value without looking for meaning, for intrinsic value; indeed, it instinctively rejects all that is not readily appraised: *der Kern, den wirft man weg.* Genuine values have been overlaid until they have fallen away like a disused limb, together with conscience. They have been scraped out until man himself has become *der ausgekratzte Mensch,* no longer real but as empty and shallow, as easily swayed, as easily manipulated as a puppet, the natural product of a superficial way of life.

(*a*) THE DIAGNOSIS

By means of the X-ray eye of the writer Böll can penetrate beneath the glittering surface of his prosperous country with its high standard of living and its material well-being to the insecure base on which its edifice has been erected. He sees what the politicians, who never look back and for whom quiet meditation is decadent, do not see, that the whole conception of West Germany is wrong, the foundations are rotten. *Ruckwärtsblicken und Nachdenken* are of primary importance. The Federal Republic must look back at the past and consider it carefully if the present is to be valid. It is insecure:

1. . . . weil seine Bewohner, seine Politiker, nicht wahrhaben wollen, **daß** am Anfang Vertreibung stand, Menschen für **Abfall erklärt,** als solcher behandelt wurden, und daß am Anfang dieses Staates ein im Abfall wühlendes Volk stand. (*Frankfurter Vorlesungen,* pp. 82–3)

> . . . because its inhabitants, its politicians, will not accept that in the beginning there was rejection, human beings were declared to be garbage, were treated as such, and that at the inception of this state was a nation rolling in garbage.

This conception of Society is appalling to a man who is as aware as Böll of the vulnerability of individual man. Having experienced the insecurity, fragility and helplessness of the individual in a world of things, he can only recoil from a materialistic society which worships these very things as all-important and treats the individual himself as an *exploitable* and then *expendable* object.

In its treatment of the individual, Böll sees little difference in essence between present-day society and the Nazi régime. The total lack of concern for individual dignity, for the situation and the predicament of others, is no less brutal than the actual atrocities of the concentration camp and no more excusable. Basic human values are eroded, human dignity is outraged, no less by the upsurge of materialism and by a sentimental view of the past than by the extermination camp and the gas chamber. And if there is such a thing as collective guilt it lies not so much in the fact that these things happened but that with the return of prosperity they should have been thrust out of sight and forgotten. It is only by looking back, by remembering that time when human beings were treated literally as expendable items, to the time of Auschwitz, Buchenwald, Dachau and Stutthof, that society can be built on sound foundations and cease from treating its misfits, its non-conformists, metaphorically as rubbish. Böll sees a society that no longer grieves, no longer remembers to what straits the denial of human dignity so recently led.

> 2. . . . eine von Abfall . . . bedrohte Gesellschaft, die noch keine Humanität hat. (Ibid., p. 82)

>   . . . a society threatened by garbage, a society completely inhumane.

Abfall and *Humanität*—these two words sum up for Böll the disease which is destroying society and the remedy from which a cure might spring.

(*b*) THE REMEDY

Humanität—humaneness. By the use of this word Böll sums up the attitude society must adopt towards its members. It demands respect for the human individual as a meaningful entity with a right to recognition and independent survival. He is more than a pawn in a political game or a cog in an economic machine. He does not exist to be manipulated. Society must accept this and patiently evolve a system which will allow those scarred by the war to recover and grow along independent, individual lines.

1. Es ist unsere Aufgabe, daran zu erinnern, daß der Mensch nicht nur existiert, um verwaltet zu werden—und daß die Zerstörungen in unserer Welt nicht nur äußerer Art sind und nicht so geringfügiger Natur, daß man sich anmaßen kann, sie in wenigen Jahren zu heilen. (*Hierzulande*, p. 134)

   It is our task to remember that a human being does not exist merely to be governed—and that the destruction in our world is not only of an external kind and not so slight that one can presume to heal it in the space of a few years.

The writer must be the representative of an institution:

2. . . . [die] die Würde des Menschen im Wort bewacht und verteidigt. (Ibid., p. 115)

   . . . which guards and defends the dignity of man.

The post-war task of Germany, in which she has failed so badly, was not just a matter of rebuilding shattered cities but of erecting a whole new social structure in which the individual would count for something: the re-establishment of human rights after the total destruction of human values by the Nazi régime.

   The agency of this regeneration should be twofold: *Kunst* and *Kirche*, the traditional guardians of the sanctity of the human spirit. In the Frankfurt Lectures Böll outlines the task of the young writer:

> 3. Das ist es, was Ihnen bevorsteht—eine Ästhetik des Humanen zu bilden, Formen und Stile zu entwickeln, die der Moral des Zustands entsprechen. (*Frankfurter Vorlesungen*, p. 87)

>> That is your task—to erect an aesthetic of the humane, to develop a form and style which live up to the morality of the object.

He enumerates the themes which should occupy the writer— recurring themes in his own work—the most important one: *love* in its widest sense.

> 4. Es bleiben noch viele Themen: Ehe, die Familie, Freund- schaft, Religion, das Essen, die Kleidung, das Geld, die Arbeit, die Zeit, ein weiteres: die Liebe. (Ibid., p. 95)

>> There still are many themes; marriage, the family, friendship, religion, food, clothes, money, work, time; yet another—love.

As well as the creation of *eine Ästhetik des Humanen*, Böll speaks too of *eine Ästhetik des Brotes in der Literatur* (p. 106). Bread is the symbol of spiritual food, a symbol for the satisfac- tion of elementary human needs, for that love for lack of which man must perish. It is also fundamental to the symbolism of the Christian Church. And it is on these themes—*Brot* and *Liebe* that Böll takes issue with the Church and specifically with his own, the Catholic Church.

> 5. . . . die Kirchen haben noch nicht begriffen, was Liebe ist, obwohl ihnen Texte zur Verfügung stehen . . . (Ibid., p. 110)

... the churches have still not grasped what love is, although they have texts at their disposal. ...

6. Im Grunde interessieren mich als Autor nur zwei Themen: die Liebe und die Religion. Für beide Themen ist im innerdeutschen Katholizismus kein Platz. (*Aufsätze Kritiken Reden*, p. 510)

> Fundamentally, only two themes interest me as a writer: love and religion. For neither theme is there any room in German Catholicism.

E. The Criticism of the Catholic Church

For Böll the Church has become just another part of the Establishment in its emphasis on form and protocol, on material things, and its proclamations are as empty and trivial as those of politicians. Doubts, despair and emptiness lie behind the eyes of the bishops as much as behind the smiles of the politicians. Because of its concern for appearances it has lost touch with the simplicity and directness of religion in its real sense. It is yet another example of the *ausgekratzte Gesellschaft*.[1] Throughout the stories and the novels we meet Catholics, both lay and professional, uneducated people and intellectuals, and Böll clearly expresses his dislike of the hypocrisy of the political-intellectual attitude, his love for the simple direct approach to religion.

Böll has a great love for his church; he finds comfort in religion; the love of Kate and Fred is based on it and even Hans Schnier likes to go to church when once the sermon is over. But the Church is failing in its duty, just as the State has done, in that it does not take into account the needs of the individual for help, for guidance, for love. The individual is denied the true bread, the real spiritual sustenance for which he craves.

1. ... Sie spüren, wie Ihr Magen knurrt; daß Sie nach Brot verlangen, nicht nach verwaschener Soziologie, ...

[1] cf. p. 34, Quote 7.

verwaschener Kulturkritik, wie man sie gemeinhin
geboten bekommt; der Magen knurrt, und das Gehirn
dürstet, dürstet bis zur Verzweiflung nach Klarheit und
Entschiedenheit . . . (*Hierzulande*, p. 42)

> . . . you feel your stomach rolling, that you want bread, not half-baked
> sociology, washed-out cultural discussions which is what you are
> offered; your stomach rolls and your brain thirsts, thirsts desperately
> for clarity and decisiveness . . .

Instead of solid sustenance he is offered brilliant rhetoric,
gesture, delicately rehearsed facial expressions, masses and
masses of words, all this practised and tried out before mirrors
and on tape-recorders before it reaches its audience. The starving congregation is presented with a faultless service in a fault-
lessly renovated church. Even in the church the emphasis is on
form rather than content; the words used are *poliert* but
ausgekrazt, polished but hollow.

2. Die deutschen Katholiken . . . haben seit Jahrzehnten
   kaum andere Sorgen gehabt als die Vervollkommnung der
   Liturgie und die Hebung des Geschmacks . . . (Ibid.,
   p. 36)

> For years German Catholics have bothered about little else but the
> perfecting of the liturgy and the raising of standards of taste . . .

The Church is so preoccupied with trivialities it neglects its
real work. Böll draws specific attention to this in his *Brief an
einen jungen Katholiker* in which the young soldier is warned of
the moral dangers to which life in the Army will expose him.
Moral danger here is equated with sexual danger, again just as
superficial an approach to the essential problem as concern with
the form of service in church. Sexual danger is a minor thing
compared with more fundamental issues.

3. Für mich, als ich in Ihrem Alter war, war es eine sittliche Gefahr hohen Grades, als der Vatikan als erster Staat mit Hitler einen Vertrag schloß; . . . Sittliche Gefahren? Es gibt deren unzählige, sobald man anfängt nachzudenken . . . (Ibid., pp. 39–40)

When I was your age a very great moral danger was involved, as far as I was concerned, when the Vatican was the first State to make a pact with Hitler. There are countless moral risks as soon as one begins to think about them . . .

4. Kein Wort über Hitler, kein Wort über Antisemitismus, über etwaige Konflikte zwischen Befehl und Gewissen. (Ibid., p. 27)

Not a word about Hitler, not a word about anti-semitism, about a possible conflict between orders and conscience.

In 1955 when the question of the re-creation of the German Army was raised, the main point that occupied the consideration of the Church was the form and quality of the prayer book which should be issued, not the moral issue as to whether West Germany should have an army at all.

5. Strapazierfähigkeit, Gediegenheit, gutes Dünndruckpapier, flexibler Leineneinband. Ich habe in Rußland zu viele Menschen sterben sehen, auf den Kampfstätten, in den Lazaretten, und ich kann diesen Satz als nichts anderes empfinden als eine teuflische Blasphemie, deren Wurzel ich in der Geschmacklerei der deutschen Katholiken suchen muß. (Ibid., pp. 38–9)

Resistance to wear and tear, sound craftmanship, good quality paper, flexible binding. I have seen so many people die in Russia, on battle fields, in field hospitals and in this sentence I can see nothing but a blasphemy which has its roots in the lack of taste of German Catholics.

The real is overlooked—*der Kern, den wirft man weg*.[1]
Catholics, if they had wished, could have blocked German re-
armament, but they had other things, for example prayer books,
to think about.

> 6. Die Katholiken als die einzige große statistische Masse
>   hätten eine Chance gehabt, dieses Volk friedfertig zu
>   erhalten. Die Chance ist verspielt. (*Aufsätze Kritiken
>   Reden*, p. 233)

>   The Catholics as the biggest single statistical group had an opportunity
>   to keep the German people as a force for peace. The chance has been
>   wasted.

But this is Böll's real indictment of the Catholic Church. The
son asks for bread and is given a stone.

> 7. Der Mensch lebt nicht vom Brot allein, aber das andere,
>   das Wort, wird ihm leider nur selten geboten, und doch
>   verlangen erstaunlich viele Menschen nach diesem Wort,
>   warten drauf, auf das Wort, das so einfach wie Brot ist,
>   das am Anfang war und am Ende sein wird. (*Hierzulande*,
>   p. 43)

>   Man does not live by bread alone, but the other, the word, is seldom
>   offered to him, and yet an amazing number of people long for this
>   word, wait for it, for the word which is as simple as bread, that was
>   at the beginning and will be at the end.

A politically involved church can never stand up for what it
knows to be right. It is forced to let more worldly considerations
cloud the moral issues. It neglects its primary duty, the feeding
of its flock.

The True Church, the Christian Society

What Böll seeks, and this is made explicit in the symbolism of
Billard um halb zehn, is a society based on a kind of primitive

[1] cf. p. 34, Quote 7.

Christianity, simple, unsophisticated, erected on a few basic principles: on love, gentleness, pity, mercy, reverence and mutual respect. Böll realizes that the majority of people do not demand much; a place of refuge, a meaningful ritual, the sympathy of someone with the capacity for love and the understanding for their basic needs. In everyone is a deep desire for confirmation and comfort. The Church should be concerned with what is to become of man and how best he can be helped to face the problem of existence. It must give *assurance* and not confuse with sterile, intellectual questionings.

Prayer is all-important. It is not only a bridge to God but also a bridge between individuals. Böll's characters find an end to isolation as they pray together, united in the communion of prayer. The observance of religious forms, of confession, the sacrament, is only made significant in love. Without this they become empty and void: *ausgekratzt*.

In religious expression, in loving communication lies the salvation of man, his survival as a dignified creature.

8. Ich gehe von der Voraussetzung aus, daß Sprache, Liebe, Gebundenheit den Menschen zum Menschen machen, daß sie den Menschen zu sich selbst, zu anderen, zu Gott in Beziehung setzen—Monolog, Dialog, Gebet. (*Frankfurter Vorlesungen*, p. 12)

I proceed from the assumption that speech, love, mutual ties, make human beings humane, that they relate man to himself, to others, to God—monologue, dialogue, prayer.

To sum up: In his essays and lectures Böll is invariably critical of contemporary society. His criticisms are based on:

1. The materialism of modern society so satisfied with the actual it never looks for the real.
2. Its inability to face up to ethical significance of the Nazi period and learn its lessons.

3. The re-creation of the Establishment ensuring the re-emerg-
   ence of the old order.
4. The inefficacy of the Catholic Church to fulfil its duty.

Böll looks to the committed writer to point the way to a
humane society, based on simple Christian values, in which the
individual has a place.

3

Böll: The Short Story Writer

In the short stories and the novels we see Böll's beliefs and concepts expressed in artistic form. We turn first to the stories. In an interview with Marcel Reich-Ranicki in 1967, Reich-Ranicki comments that Böll has written few short stories in recent years. Böll replies:

> 1. Ich möchte die Kurzgeschichte gern wieder zum „Mittelpunkt" machen . . . Die Kurzgeschichte ist immer noch die schönste aller Prosaformen. (*Aufsätze Kritiken Reden*, p. 510)

> I should like the short story to become once more the main vehicle of my work . . . the short story is still the most pleasing form of all prose writing.

Here we see Böll's fondness for the particular form of writing which first gave powerful expression to the emotions stirred by the horrors of war.

Although it is not possible to group the stories into complete chronological groups—*Als der Krieg ausbrach* and *Als der Krieg zu Ende War* were written as late as 1961–2, but their subject-matter places them among the first stories—a change of approach, a shift of emphasis, makes it feasible to place them into two categories:

A. *Kriegs-Trümmer- und Heimkehrer Literatur:* stories concerned with the catastrophe of the war and its chaotic aftermath: *the human condition experienced.*

B. *The Satires:* Stories commenting on the society which has emerged from the war: *the human condition observed,*

Böll's approach to his subject-matter changes and becomes more subtle as he gains in stature as a writer, but the theme remains the same from the start: *the confrontation of the individual with a monster of a world*; the helplessness of that individual in the face of abstract power. The early stories are an outcry in the Borchert manner and have the directness, the realism and the agony of a passionate protest against the inhumanity of war. Later stories are shot through with laughter as the human situation is observed at some remove, viewed from without rather than within. Satire replaces outrage and indignation, but the warning is always there. The dangers threatening the human spirit remain and become even more dangerous as they grow less tangible, less obviously menacing, lurking beneath the surface of a settled and prosperous society. The threat is ever present; the abstract monster once manifest as war is replaced by society itself, and is much more nebulous. Böll refuses to be lulled into a false sense of security and attacks this hydra-headed monster in all its manifestations, from the merely shallow and stupid to the cruel and dangerous. The stories mock social pretentiousness, snobbishness and self-satisfied smugness, and expose more bitterly the greed, injustice and indifference of a society without conscience whose god is success and which recognizes none but its own kind.

A. Kriegs-Trümmer- und Heimkehrer Literatur: The Early Stories

The stories which fall naturally into this group are written mostly between 1947 and 1950 and are characterized by immediacy of impact, a directness, an urgency and a vivid realism. The horror and wastefulness of war, its devastating and crippling effect on the human spirit, is sharply exposed as Böll's spotlight falls on dugout and shellhole, on hastily converted hospital accommodation, on the anxious living, the incredulous dying and the shapeless dead. They have a common theme—the senseless disruption and destruction of individual personal lives by a vast impersonal machine.

Typically Böll expresses his theme in the very form of the stories. Many of them have an 'unfinished' ending, the last sentence trails away into a series of dots:

1. „Milch" sagte ich leise . . . (*Wanderer, kommst du nach Spa . . .* p. 43)

    'Milk,' I said softly . . .

2. und als sie hochstiegen, wußten wir plötzlich, daß wir nie mehr wiederkommen würden, nie mehr . . . (Ibid., p. 34)

    and when they were airborne we suddenly knew that we would never come back again, never . . .

The reader is left with the feeling that each story is only one aspect of a many-sided obscenity, a fragment of a larger story that will never end. The happenings will continue to have their effect in the unknown, questionable future.

3. Da wußte ich, daß der Krieg niemals zu Ende sein würde, niemals solange noch irgendwo eine Wunde blutete, die er geschlagen hat. (Ibid., p. 69)

    Then I knew that the war would never be over, never as long as a single wound inflicted by it continued to bleed.

The frequent presentation of the stories in the first person draws the reader into the narrative and he realizes the universality of the experiences described. A personal relationship is set up. He becomes involved and concerned that there should be so much suffering to so little purpose; he becomes involved directly in the effort to find a solution. The title of the above story, *Die Botschaft*, sums up the function of the majority of stories in this section: the conveying of a message which he must perceive and interpret if the human spirit is to survive the catastrophe of total war. Complete involvement and the awareness of our common responsibilities for the future is the first vital lesson to be learned.

> 4. Es gibt nichts, was uns nichts angeht, das heißt positiv: alles geht uns etwas an. (*Hierzulande*, p. 61)
>
>> There is nothing that does not concern us; that means, expressed positively, everything is our concern.

(a) WAR, THE ABSTRACT POWER

War is summed up by Böll in blunt, coarse language in case anyone should harbour the romantic illusion that it is sweet and noble to die for one's country. The soldier in *Trunk in Petöcki* tries to forget it as he gets drunk for a few hours in a vain attempt to escape. There is no escape. In the end he must leave the warmth and peace of the dimly lighted room. He must walk along the tree-lined road to the station which will lead him back to the war, to the perpetual struggle for survival.

In the story written much later *Als der Krieg ausbrach* Böll relates the telephone conversation between a soldier and his girl-friend. War has just broken out; they are tense, fearful, disturbed; the future is suddenly less predictable. Into their inarticulate conversation breaks the irate voice of a high-ranking officer concerned only with the weapons of war.

> 5. . . . und ich sagte: ,,Ach, Marie, es ist Krieg, Krieg",— und sie sagte: ,,Nein". Ich sagte: ,,Doch", dann blieb es

eine halbe Minute still, und sie sagte: „Soll ich kommen?",
and noch bevor ich spontan, meiner Stimmung gehor-
chend: „Ja, ja, ja" gesagt hatte, schrie die Stimme eines,
wahrscheinlich ziemlich hohen Offiziers: „Munition
brauchen wir, wir brauchen dringend Munition". Das
Mädchen sagte: „Bist du noch da?" Der Offizier brüllte
„Schweinerei". (*Als der Krieg ausbrach*, p. 11)

> ... and I said, 'Oh, Marie, it's war, war'— and she said, 'No.' I said,
> 'But it is,' then there was silence for half a minute and she said, 'Shall
> I come?' and before I could answer spontaneously 'Yes, oh yes,' the
> voice of an officer, probably a high-ranking one, screamed, 'We need
> ammunition, we need ammunition urgently.' The girl said, 'Are you
> still there?' The officer roared, 'What the hell's going on?'

War is here the impersonal intruder which invades the private
life of the individual, ruthlessly imposes itself between him and
those closest to him, and effectively cuts off his former existence.
Similarly, in *Die Postkarte*, the arrival of the summons to a
fortnight's military training which lasts for the whole of the war
transforms the life of the recipient. He survives, indeed he is
more fortunate than many of Böll's characters who return from
the war and are unable to get to grips with life again. His wife
has kept open his position with his firm; he still has promotion
prospects, he has prospered materially. But it has all gone sour,
his life remains unfulfilled. He is in the wrong role, part of the
acquisitive materialistic society.

(b) THE INDIVIDUAL, THE HELPLESS VICTIM

The civilian becomes a soldier, the individual becomes a cog
in a vast machine. He relinquishes all personal responsibility,
and merely carries out the commands of others. He is not required to think, he functions mindlessly. He is taken to the air-
port in a truck each day, *Damals in Odessa*. If the weather is
fine he will be flown to the Crimea, if it is foggy he will be taken
back to the barracks. Either way, he will have no part in the

decision. The effect on the individual is demoralizing. If he is
not in the battle zone he is kept waiting, endlessly waiting, his
time filled with monotonous, senseless tasks.

1. Es war noch hell, als wir Stiefel von Eisenbahnwaggons
   auf Lastwagen luden, aber als wir Stiefel von Lastwagen
   auf Eisenbahnwaggons luden, war es dunkel, und es war
   immer noch dunkel, als wir wieder Stiefel von Eisenbahnwaggons auf Lastwagen luden, dann war es wieder hell,
   und wir luden Heuballen von Lastwagen auf Eisenbahnwaggons, und es war immer noch hell, und wir luden
   Heuballen von Lastwagen auf Eisenbahnwaggons; dann
   aber war es wieder dunkel, und genau doppelt so lange, wie
   wir Heuballen von Lastwagen auf Eisenbahnwaggons
   geladen hatten, luden wir Heuballen von Eisenbahnwaggons auf Lastwagen. (*Als der Krieg Ausbrach*, p. 12)

> It was still light when we loaded boots from the railway trucks on to
> lorries, but when we were loading boots from lorries into railway
> trucks it was dark, and it was still dark when we loaded boots from
> the railway trucks into the lorries again, then it was light again and
> we were loading bales of hay from lorries into railway trucks, and it
> was still light, and we were still loading bales of hay from lorries into
> railway trucks, but then it was dark again and twice as long as we
> had loaded bales of hay from lorries into railway trucks we loaded
> bales of hay from trucks into lorries.

(*c*) FEAR

If he is at the front he has the additional burden of fear, sharp
animal fear, because he knows he is trapped, groping in darkness over pitted earth.

2. Angst wurde in mir wach und breitete sich immer mehr
   aus . . . (*Wanderer, kommst du nach Spa* . . . p. 91)

3. . . . um so mehr auch blähte sich in mir die Angst
   (Ibid., p. 91)

4. . . . wir waren erst seit acht Wochen beim Militär und hatten viel Angst . . . (Ibid., p. 30)

5. . . . und manchmal hoben wir gleichzeitig unsere Köpfe und blickten uns ängstlich an . . . (Ibid., p. 89)

Fear stirred in me and spread out further and further . . .

. . . fear swelled within me more and more.

. . . we had only been soldiers for eight weeks and were very frightened . . .

. . . and sometimes we raised our heads at the same time and stared fearfully at one another . . .

Not least of his fears is that of physical pain, inglorious, squalid, unheroic but real. Physical pain[1] and violent death,[2] all too vividly described by Böll, constitute his everyday experience. Young healthy bodies become in a moment pieces of mutilated flesh. The young soldier in *Wanderer, kommst du nach Spa . . .* who has left school only a short time before, suddenly becomes aware of his pitiful body when its bandages are removed before an operation.

6. sie hatten mich ausgewickelt, und ich hatte keine Arme mehr, auch kein rechtes Bein mehr, und ich fiel ganz plötzlich nach hinten, weil ich mich nicht aufstützen konnte; ich schrie; . . . (Ibid., p. 43)

They had unwrapped me and I had no arms and I had no right leg either, and I fell back quite suddenly because I could not prop myself up; I screamed . . .

The horror lies in the sudden falling back of the helpless trunk, the anguished helpless cry.

[1] *Wiedersehen mit Drüng, Wanderer, kommst du nach Spa . . . Lohengrins Tod*
[2] *Die Essenholer, Wiedersehen in der Allee, In der Finsternis*

In *Wiedersehen in der Allee* we experience the abrupt termination of a human life, of a reasonable, cultured, intelligent, individual who has tried to carry some little civilized comfort and behaviour into the harsh reality of a dug-out.

7. Hecker wandte sich mit einer erschreckenden Plötzlichkeit um, lächelte mich kurz und selig an, dann legte er seine Zigarette auf die Böschung und sank in sich zusammen, ganz langsam fiel er hintenüber . . . und es quoll Blut heraus und eine fürchterliche gelblichweiße Masse, von der ich glauben mußte, daß es sein Gehirn war; es floß und floß und ich dachte mit starrem Schrecken nur: woher kommt diese unendliche Masse Blut, aus seinem Kopf allein? (Ibid., p. 102)

Hecker turned round with frightening suddenness, smiled briefly and happily, then he laid his cigarette on the parapet and collapsed, he fell over quite slowly . . . and blood flowed out, and a horrible yellowish white mass which I realized must be his brain; it flowed on and on, frozen with horror I could only think: where is all this endless blood coming from, is it just from his head?

Unpleasant, uncomfortable, tasteless realism for those who would stress the nobility and heroism of a patriotic death; more violent and less subtle than any of Böll's later writing but alive with Böll's conviction that war stories must be a crying out. War must not be treated with cool composure. No one who reads these stories, not even those for whom this war is merely pages in a history book can remain unmoved by the senselessness, wastefulness and inhumanity of Böll's war.

(*d*) INSECURITY

The tenuous hold on life of the front-line soldier who at any moment sees the world blown apart and his friends obliterated is shared to some extent by his fellow-soldiers, perpetually on the move from place to place; although external reality for the

latter does not disintegrate literally, it changes so often that he
no longer feels any relationship to it and the only reality for him
is himself. His whole world revolves round railway stations in
unnamed desolate little towns in the middle of nowhere. All
roads lead to the station and from the station back into the war.
In the end all places are the same. The individual is unable to
build up any sort of contact with things outside himself. He is
alone, insecure in a dark alien world, and has an inner compul-
sion to keep on the move. This desolation speaks from the
final words of a wounded soldier in a hospital compound, for-
bidden to fraternize with a Russian child. When the child dis-
appears in the falling snow he forces himself to move too.

1. Ich ging, weil ich doch irgendwohin gehen mußte. Man
   muß doch irgendwohin gehen, das muß man doch.
   Man kann ja nicht stehenbleiben und sich zuschneien
   lassen. Irgendwohin muß man gehen, auch wenn man
   verwundet ist in einem fremden, schwarzen, sehr dunklen
   Land . . . (*Wanderer, kommst du nach Spa* . . . p. 57)

   I went, because I had to go somewhere after all. You've got to go
   somewhere, you just have to. You can't just stand still, can you, and
   let snow cover you up. You have to go somewhere, even if you're
   wounded in an alien country . . .

This is a feeling shared by a whole generation in the chaotic
post-war world, by people who do not fit in, cannot find their
place and are kept on the run by a cold and unsympathetic
society. The life of the young black-marketeer in *Kumpel mit
dem langen Haar*, has been lived in a constant state of tension
and insecurity. Nowhere can he feel safe, nowhere can he settle
down.

2. Wo würde ich diese Nacht schlafen, dachte ich . . . wo
   einmal wieder nur etwas zur Ruhe kommen. (Ibid., p. 15)

3. Eine feste Bleibe habe ich nicht. (Ibid., p. 15)

4. Ach, ich hatte keine Freunde in dieser stillen Stadt, die mir so fremd war wie alle anderen. (Ibid., p. 16)

> Where would I sleep tonight, I thought . . . where shall I ever be able to settle down again.
>
> I haven't got a permanent place to live.
>
> Oh, I had no friends in this quiet town, which was as alien to me as all the others.

(e) ALIENATION

The final assault on the individual however comes from within. Demoralized by his inability to make real contact with the world around him, dehumanized by his role of helpless pawn in a game whose pattern never emerges and which he does not know how to play, he finds he can no longer hold onto his essential being, to himself. He gazes at himself as at yet another object to which he has no relationship.

1. Ich lag auf dem Operationstisch und sah mich selbst ganz deutlich, aber sehr klein, zusammengeschrumpft, oben in dem klaren Glas der Glühbirne, winzig und weiß, ein schmales, mullfarbenes Paketchen wie ein außergewöhnlich subtiler Embryo: das war also ich da oben. (*Wanderer, kommst du nach Spa . . .*, p. 42)

> I lay on the operating table and saw myself quite clearly but very small, shrunken, up there in the glass of the electric bulb, white and tiny, a narrow dun-coloured bundle like an unusually well-formed embryo; so that was me up there, was it?

He regards himself curiously and is surprised to discover that it is himself lying remote and distant, waiting indifferently for something to happen to him. This is a state of alienation. In *Wiedersehen mit Drüng* he speaks of a stranger, adding as an afterthought that this stranger must evidently be himself. Not only is he separated from his own entity but also from the events in which he has so recently been taking part.

2. Was vor einer Stunde geschehen war, sah ich jetzt sehr deutlich, aber fern, als blickte ich vom Rande unseres Erdballs in eine andere Welt, die durch einen himmelweiten glasigklaren Abgrund von der unseren geschieden war. Dort sah ich jemand, der ich selbst sein mußte . . . diese trostlose Silhouette . . . ich sah diesen Fremden, der ich selbst sein mußte . . . (Ibid., p. 82)

> The events of an hour ago I saw very clearly, but at a distance, as if I was looking from the edge of our earth into another world, separated from ours by a vast abyss, clear as glass. There I saw somebody, who must have been myself . . . this inconsolable silhouette . . . I saw this stranger which must have been myself. . . .

He is only a shadow, a despairing shadow separated by an abyss from the warmth and consolation of real contact. The image of the *abyss* as a symbol of complete isolation occurs often in these spiritually desolate stories.

3. . . . ich fürchtete jeden Augenblick in einem Abgrund zu versinken . . . (Ibid., p. 70)

> . . . every moment I was frightened I would sink into the abyss . . .

4. . . . ich hatte das schreckliche Gefühl, am Ende der Welt wie vor einem unendlichen Abgrund zu stehen, als sei ich verdammt, hineingezogen zu werden . . . (Ibid., p. 67)

> . . . I had the terrible feeling of standing at the end of the world as if in front of an abyss, as if I were condemned to be drawn into it . . .

5. So war ich oft am Rande der Wirklichkeit einhergegangen
mit der Sicherheit eines Trunkenen, der auf der schmalen
Kante eines Abgrundes seinen Weg macht . . . (Ibid.,
p. 72)

I had often walked along the edge of reality with the sureness of a
drunken man making his way along the edge of an abyss . . .

The individual is separated in both space and time. Time,
which is to play a specific role in later novels, already begins to
present itself as a problem in the short stories. Under the
pressures of war, time becomes a precious and all too limited
commodity. The transcience of man is underlined when each
moment may bring a complete cessation of time as it is
experienced by the individual. His life slips away with frightening speed. Böll is acutely aware of passing seconds, of time
seeping away (*die vertropfende Zeit*). In *Wiedersehen in der
Allee* the thudding bullets from the sniper's gun emphasize
this.

6. Zwischendurch mahnte uns das Scharfschützengeschoß,
daß die Zeit unbarmherzig vertropfte . . . (Ibid., p. 98)

Spasmodically the bullets of the sniper reminded us that time
was mercilessly dripping away . . .

Because nothing feels stable or real, neither in time nor in
space, the individual is pervaded not only by a feeling of hopelessness but also of *indifference*. It no longer matters to him that
this is *his* life. He begins to feel that he is not living but playing
a game. He is a stranger to himself, as a character is to an
actor, and the events in which he is taking part and which
constitute his life appear to him as an inarticulate and miserable
game. Life is remote and nothing to do with him—a flickering
film on a flat screen.

7. . . . die Erinnerung lief in mir ab wie ein Bildstreifen, an dem ich keinen Teil hatte. (Ibid., p. 82)

> . . . time past ran through my mind, like a strip cartoon in which I had no part.

Here we see the start of a theme which is to occupy Böll in his later writings. Here he expresses it intuitively as man's basic dilemma: *man in isolation, life as a game or play* in which it is so easy to be cast in the wrong role.

8. Dieses Leben, dachte ich, ist nicht mein Leben. Ich muß dieses Leben spielen, und ich spiele es schlecht. (Ibid., p. 74)

> This life, I thought, is not my life. I have to act this life and I am doing it badly.

The image of the *Ich* drifting aimlessly in the dark with nothing tangible to cling to is caught in the short story *Aufenthalt in X*. A soldier wakens in the early morning to feel himself quite dissociated from his physical self—a gently rocking ship afloat in a swaying vacuum.

9. Als ich wach wurde, erfüllte mich das Bewußtsein fast vollkommener Verlorenheit; ich schien in der Dunkelheit zu schwimmen wie in einem träge fließenden Gewässer, dessen Strömung ohne Ziel war; wie ein Leichnam, den die Welle endgültig an die unbarmherzige Oberfläche gespült hat, trudelte ich leise schwankend hin und her in dieser Finsternis, die ohne Halt war. Meine Glieder spürte ich nicht, sie waren ohne Zusammenhang mit mir, auch meine Sinne waren erloschen; es war nichts zu sehen, nichts zu hören, kein Geruch bot mir Anhalt . . . (Ibid., p. 72)

When I woke up I was filled by a feeling of being almost completely
lost. I seemed to be swimming in the darkness as in a lazily flowing
stretch of water, flowing in no particular direction; like a corpse
which the waves have finally floated to the merciless surface I drifted
backwards and forwards in the darkness, with nothing to hold on to.
I could not feel my limbs, they had no connection with me, even my
senses were extinguished; there was nothing to see, nothing to hear,
no smell by which I could orientate myself . . .

Ohne Ziel . . . ohne Halt, aimless and with *no fixed point of
reference*, this is how Böll sees the individual in his early stories,
a view which remains one of his fundamental conceptions of
the human condition. But Böll is not a nihilist. Just as he
thought it necessary to describe the shattered cities and
destruction wrought by the war, he felt it important to show
individual man in his extremity so that he might at least
indicate some possibility of happiness and fulfilment. He
presents us with the actual state of affairs in order that we
might be able to decipher reality and find some basis for hope.
Even in the first stories we can see the beginnings of hope.

(f) HALT UND ZIEL

Böll is a Catholic and his religion is important to him. He
cannot accept, therefore, what his investigations into human
existence would apparently suggest—that life is meaningless
and that man is completely alone. He sees the basic need of the
individual as some point of reference and some ultimate goal:
a meaningful relationship with another human being to alleviate
present loneliness and the promise of an ultimately happier
existence.

Love in all its senses is the bridge by which man can span the
abyss between himself and others; through love he is redeemed.
It may be personal: the love of a man for a woman,[1] the bond
of friendship,[2] family loyalty[3] or it may be impersonal: selfless

[1] *Kumpel mit dem langen Haar.*
[2] *Wiedersehen in der Allee.*
[3] *Lohengrins Tod.*

devotion to others.[1] It may find expression in love of God through communion and prayer.[2] There is something of eternity in the handclasp of another human being; in love, friendship and devotion we touch something imperishable. We have gained the elusive bond of affection, we can escape the prison of ourselves and find some kind of objective validity. Sexual love is more fully developed in the novels, for example the dependence of Fred Bogner on Kate, of Hans Schnier on Maria, but it is there in the first stories too. In *Aufenthalt in X* the narrator is overwhelmed by his extreme loneliness and his consequent feeling of the unreality of everything.

1. Ich war ganz allein in dieser Stadt, diese Menschen gehörten nicht zu mir, diese Bäumchen waren aus Spielzeugschachteln ausgepackt und auf diese sanften grauen Bürgersteige geklebt, und der Himmel schwebte über allem wie ein lautloses Luftschiff, das stürzen würde . . . (*Wanderer, kommst du nach Spa . . .* p. 75)

   I was completely alone in this town, these people had nothing to do with me, these little trees had been unpacked from toy boxes and stuck onto these soft grey pavements and the sky hovered over everything like a noiseless airship about to fall . . .

Suddenly he sees an opportunity to make *human* contact, to prove he really exists. He sees a girl standing beneath the trees.

2. Ich faßte ihren Arm, einen menschlichen Arm, unsere Handflächen krampften sich ineinander, unsere Finger fanden sich und schlossen sich zusammen, während wir in dieser unbekannten Stadt in eine unbekannte Straße gingen. (Ibid., p. 75)

   I seized her arm, a human arm, our hands met, clenched convulsively, our fingers found one another and intertwined, as we walked along an unknown street in an unknown town.

   [1] *Wiedersehen mit Drüng, Wanderer, kommst du nach Spa . . .*
   [2] *Kerzen für Maria.*

The young black-marketeer *Kumpel mit dem langen Haar* who has no place to stay, no permanent address, and follows the equally lonely girl onto the train, feels the same desperate need for physical contact.

> 3. Ach, könnte ich doch mein Gesicht in diesen schwarzen Haaren verbergen. Nichts, sonst nichts . . . (Ibid., p. 15)

> Oh, if only I could just hide my face in her black hair. Nothing, nothing more . . .

When they get off the train he offers to take her home.

> 4. Da blieb sie plötzlich stehen. Es war unter einer Lampe. Sie blickte mich ganz starr an und sagte mit gepreßtem Mund: „Wüßte ich nur wohin?" . . . Wir gingen langsam aus der Stadt heraus und krochen schließlich in einen Heuschober . . . Als es kühl wurde, gegen Morgen, kroch ich ganz nahe zu ihr, und sie deckte einen Teil ihres dünnen Mäntelchens über mich. (Ibid., p. 16)

> Then suddenly she stopped. It was under a lamp. She stared at me and said, her mouth tight, 'If only I knew where to?' . . . We walked slowly out of the town and finally crawled into a haystack . . . When it grew cold towards morning I crept close to her and she wrapped part of her thin coat round me.

Both are lonely, neither has found a place in society and together they make a pathetic but necessary attempt to find some refuge in a remote and indifferent world.

Brüderliche Liebe which Böll finds lacking in the contemporary world is instanced in the stories by Lohengrin's devotion to his younger brothers. Selfless devotion and love for one's fellow-man outside the bonds of family is reflected in the same story, in the soothing hands of the nun who attends to Lohengrin, in the tired face of Birgler, *Wanderer, kommst du nach Spa* . . . as he gives the dying boy a cigarette, in the gentle eyes of Dina, *Wiedersehen mit Drüng*. All are there to *help* and *comfort*, to *minister*, to love in its fullest sense. They are sharply contrasted with the woman in the train who tells the guard that the girl and boy have no tickets, with the woman who buys from Elsa Baskoleit's father and will not listen to his grief for his dead daughter. They represent the cold, non-loving, abstract world.

Love is a refuge in a bleak world, a relationship which alleviates isolation. In some of the early stories Böll takes one further step which is peculiar to this period; the concept of ultimate happiness beyond death where loneliness and separation come to an end. A simple, conventional approach to death and life after death is made. There is a release from heavy burdens,[1] an end to all fear,[2] a reunion with loved ones.[3] The immediate pre-death state is one of intense fear, but this passes away. The provision party, blown to bits by a direct hit, is greeted by a great voice full of love and the mutilated body they bear is made whole. The man at the grave whose sweetheart has died sees a bright plain before him on which the one he mourns is standing, smiling and repeating his former agonized words in another sense. In *Wiedersehen mit Drüng* the two men go forward into brightness from the hut in which they have died; the door is the door to light and knowledge. A similar bright golden light shines at the end of the avenue in *Wiedersehen in der Allee* as the young soldier follows the silhouette of his officer who has just died.

But this conventional solution has no follow-up in Böll's more sophisticated work. He subsequently sees redemption through love and entry into the kingdom as an ever-present possibility. The solution of the early stories offers consolation

---

[1] *Steh auf, steh doch auf, Die Essenholer.*
[2] *Wiedersehen mit Drüng.*
[3] *Wiedersehen in der Allee.*

for the brutal and arbitrary severance of innocent life. Later Böll offers a less conventional solution: for those able to experience love, then security, even immortality, need not wait upon death. Through love we can penetrate to the fullness of reality at any moment. If time has no meaning, then death or age as a specific point in time is not a prerequisite for revelation. Such moments stand outside time and the kingdom is gained from which one can apprehend the real and learn to live.

The redeeming power of love, its illuminating and liberating effect upon the human spirit, is sensitively illustrated in Böll's delicate story of adolescence *Im Tal der donnernden Hufe*. In the adolescent Paul, Böll shows man at his most vulnerable, thus intensifying the predicament of the emerging individual, idealistic and rebellious, in confrontation with an indifferent world. Paul sees society as degenerate, degrading everything it touches. His boyhood paradise—the valley of thundering hooves—is no longer accessible; the security of childhood has gone. Tormented by sexual desire which he has been brought up by that society and its church to consider sinful, longing to make a flamboyant gesture, he toys with the idea of suicide. Imprisoned in his own loneliness he cannot bring himself to confess to the indifferent ear of a world-weary priest. He does not know how to begin to come to terms with a society where genuine emotion is inhibited by moral conventions which distort and debase what he knows is good. This society, with its hypocritical church, its abstract God and its fossilized morality, he can only reject.

Through his experience of love with Mirzowa he comes to a new awareness. Sexual love is revealed as a sacrament, an essential part of love, a way of healing and rebirth. Sexual and spiritual love are inextricably interwoven. In his essay *Brief an einen jungen Katholiken*, Böll writes:

5. . . . es mir unmöglich ist, das, was man irrigerweise die körperliche Liebe nennt zu verachten; sie ist die Substanz

eines Sakraments . . .; es gibt nie rein die körperliche, nie rein die andere; beide enthalten immer eine Beimischung der anderen, sei es auch nur eine winzige. Wir sind weder reine Geister noch reine Körper . . . (*Hierzulande*, p. 29)

> . . . it is impossible for me to despise what is erroneously called physical love; it is the substance of a sacrament . . .; there is no such thing as purely physical love or purely spiritual love, both contain an element of the other even if only a tiny one. We are neither pure spirits nor pure bodies . . .

This essay statement is translated into the image of the complicated pattern of red and white tiles in the church where Paul waits at the confessional; the theme of the story finds vivid and immediate artistic expression.

With and through Mirzowa he has had a glimpse of another valley, he has found a new concept of religion, a new morality. He has discovered the way to enter the kingdom from the shelter of which he can make his protest against society and his gesture against its idols. He turns his revolver away from himself, away from the insignificant jars of jam defiantly taken from the cupboard and turns it towards the hanging beer advertisement, symbol of a materialistic, insensitive society. He can then say quite truthfully to the incomprehending representative of that society, the policeman who demands his address

6. Ich wohne im Tal der donnernden Hufe . . . Ich wohne in Jerusalem. (*Als der Krieg ausbrach*, p. 186)

> I live in the valley of thundering hooves . . . I dwell in Jerusalem.

To sum up: In the first stories we have much that is to form the theme of Böll's work as a whole:

1. A protest against the violation of individual existence by an external force.

2. The individual as a victim exploited by this force.
3. His isolation, insecurity and consequent alienation.
4. An unsophisticated attempt at a solution.

B. The Satires

In the satires, Böll approaches similar themes from another standpoint. The problems of existence, no longer threatened so immediately, are examined at a greater remove. Böll is still involved in the search for solutions, but he is able to stand back and view things in a more relaxed, more objective manner. He finds satire a sharper weapon with which to achieve his ends. To make ridiculous, to probe the sensitive spots, is to be more effective. Ears grow deaf with too much lamentation so Böll, with his quick eye for the pretentious and the absurd, clothes his criticism in humour. For all his moral seriousness, Böll cannot long remain solemn. This gives the balanced view that is the essential Böll.

Stressing the humanity of humour he says:

1. Aber wir wollen es so sehen, wie es ist, mit einem menschlichen Auge, das normalerweise nicht ganz trocken und nicht ganz naß ist, sondern feucht . . . (*Hierzulande,* p. 133)

   But we will look at things as they are, with a human eye which is normally not completely dry nor completely wet but damp . . .

2. . . . und das lateinische Wort für Feuchtigkeit ist: Humor. (Ibid., p. 130)

   . . . and the Latin word for dampness is humour.

In the satirical short story Böll is at his best. It is the ideal vehicle for the lightning sortie against the conceits of a self-satisfied, prosperous society. We are charmed by the *selige*

Asozialen, the pure in heart, the odd men out, the innocents who live their own different lives in unlikely occupations. We laugh comfortably at the startling literary success of Bodo Belgelmann *Die unsterbliche Theodora*, the experiences of the research student *Im Lande der Rujuks*, the family with a weakness for homeless animals *Unberechenbare Gäste*. Our laughter is uninhibited and the point is taken. The stories are valid on this level and a refreshing change from the earlier ones. But there is another serious level on which they function and which gives no cause for amusement. Böll will not allow us to forget that there are some things which are no subject for amusement.

> 3. . . . daß es Dinge gibt, bei denen kein Anlaß für Humor besteht. (Ibid., p. 133)
>
> . . . that there are some things which do not give rise to humour.

Satire is not entirely absent from the early stories. *Wanderer, kommst du nach Spa . . .* provides an example of this approach. In the school, where children are taught the virtues of heroism and patriotism beneath the pictures of military leaders, and to write on the board 'When you come to Sparta, tell them how bravely and gloriously we died', lies the broken body of a boy who has died miserably, ingloriously and in vain, and whose life has been cut off as abruptly as his writing. In *Kumpel mit dem langen Haar*, society makes outcasts of those forced to live on their wits by society itself. In these two stories we see the shift of emphasis from war as monster to society as monster.

(a) SOCIETY

In his address on the occasion of the *Woche der Brüderlichkeit*, Böll refers to a newspaper picture he has seen, shortly after the end of the war in Biafra:

> 1. Wenige Tage nach der Beendigung des Brüderkriegs dort habe ich ein Bild von brutaler Obszönität gesehen, einen

wieder in Gang gesetzten Bohrturm, der triumphierend
seine Kolben in den Schoß der Erde stieß. Dieses Bild
sagte: „Es ist alles wieder normal", was bedeutet: die
alten Herrschaftsverhältnisse sind wieder hergestellt. Der
alte Rahmen wieder festgefügt. (*Kölner Stadt-Anzeiger*,
9 March 1970)

> Shortly after the end of the civil war I saw a picture of brutal
> obscenity, a rig in action again plunging its drill deep into the earth.
> This picture proclaimed: 'Everything is back to normal' which
> means the old relationship of masters and men is re-established.
> The old structure has been set up again.

Everything is all right again, that is, everything is *as it was
before*. Böll is saying this in 1970. We find a similar statement
in the short story *Geschäft ist Geschäft* (1950)

> 2. Es gab sogar wieder Wochenkarten bei der Straßenbahn,
>   das beste Zeichen, daß wirklich alles in Ordnung war.
>   (*Wanderer, kommst du nach Spa* . . . p. 133)

> > There were even weekly tickets on the trams again, a sure sign that
> > everything was in order.

The initial mistake of society lies in its desire to have everything as it was before, to sweep the war under the carpet, to dis-
claim all responsibility, to play Blind Man's Buff. There are
those returning soldiers who have lived through the war without emotion, who have come through unscathed mentally if
not physically, shrugging off personal responsibility and feeling
rather fine fellows after all.

> 3. . . . man erzählte von Orden, Verwundungen, Heldentaten
>   und fand, daß man schließlich doch ein Prachtbengel sei:
>   man hatte letzten Endes nichts als seine Pflicht getan.
>   (Ibid., p. 133)

. . . they talked about their decorations, battle scars, deeds of heroism and discovered that they were rather fine fellows. They had only
done their duty, after all.

In certain social circles the war is being dismissed laconically
as rather a bore:

4. In den Jahren 1939 bis 1945 hatten wir Krieg. Im Krieg
   wird gesungen, geschossen, geredet, gekämpft, gehungert
   und gestorben—und es werden Bomben geschmissen—
   lauter unerfreuliche Dinge, mit deren Erwähnung ich
   meine Zeitgenossen in keiner Weise langweilen will.
   (*Nicht nur zur Weihnachtszeit*, p. 10)

   In the years 1939 to 1945 we were at war. In war there is singing,
   shooting, talking, starving, fighting, dying—and bombs are dropped
   —most displeasing things, and I will not bore my contemporaries by
   talking about them.

This is the attitude pinpointed by Böll in the satire *Nicht nur
zur Weihnachtszeit*. For Tante Milla, wife of a wealthy in-
dustrialist, the war has meant only one thing—it has spoiled
her Christmasses.

5. Denn der Krieg wurde von meiner Tante Milla nur
   registriert als eine Macht, die schon Weihnachten 1939
   anfing, ihren Weihnachtsbaum zu gefährden. (Ibid., p. 10)

   For Aunt Milla the war only registered as a disturbance which began
   as early as 1939 to put her Christmas tree in danger.

After the war she is able to have her celebrations again but
suffers a nervous collapse when, with the arrival of Twelfth
Night, the tree must be burned and the decorations put away.
She shows no improvement until everything is restored and
Christmas celebrations take place nightly. The descriptions of

Christmas Eve in July behind drawn curtains in front of built-up fires, of attempts to divert Tante Milla by an occasional burst of *Komm, lieber Mai* instead of *Stille Nacht*, of the wholesale order for Christmas trees, anvil-beating dwarfs and whispering angels, are hilarious. The endless difficulties involved in the deception are investigated by Böll with all his flair for thinking things out to their logical end. The wider implications are clear. The insistence that all should be as it used to be (*daß alles so sein sollte wie früher*), that the unpleasant time of no Christmas trees should be forgotten, has a catastrophic effect on the family as such an attitude of mind must have on the attempt to create a responsible society.

> 6. . . . man zündete die Kerzen an, ließ die Zwerge hämmern, den Engel flüstern, man sang, aß Gebäck—und alles schien in Ordnung zu sein. (Ibid., p. 17)

> . . . the candles were lit, the dwarfs hammered, the angel whispered, we sang and ate—and everything seemed to be in order.

Everything *seems* to be in order but it is only superficial. In reality all is very much out of order and will continue to be so until the war and the Hitler period has been acknowledged and expiated. The coming to terms with the past (*Die Vergangenheit bewältigen*) is a major theme in Böll's later work. The equivocal attitude towards Hitler, the refusal to face facts, undermines attempts to begin again as a real society. An elderly lady writes to Broadcasting House suggesting a programme on dogs. *Doktor Murkes gesammeltes Schweigen.*

> 7. Hitler hatte bestimmt seine Nachteile: wenn man alles glauben kann, was man so hört, war er ein garstiger Mensch, aber eins hatt'er: er hatte ein Herz für Hunde und tat etwas für sie. (Ibid., p. 101)

BÖLL: THE SHORT STORY WRITER 69

> Hitler had his disadvantages of course: if one can believe all one hears he was rather a nasty man, but one thing in his favour—he liked dogs and did something for them.

In Ireland, Böll is questioned about Hitler, *Irisches Tagebuch*:

8. „Sag mal," sagte er leise, „Hitler—war—glaube ich—kein so schlechter Mann, nur ging er—so glaube ich—ein wenig zu weit." (*Irisches Tagebuch*, p. 46)

> 'Tell me,' he said softly, 'Hitler wasn't—such a bad man, just that— I mean—he went a bit too far.'

This attitude of mind Böll attacks ruthlessly. A society which thinks along those lines will never be in order again.

The second, more serious, mistake of society lies in its treatment of the individual—and in this it shows itself to be as ruthless as war. War required obedient soldiers, efficient cogs in the war machine. Society requires obedient members, efficient units in the service of the economy and the state. What freedom there appears to be is a mirage. The 'sie' of society, the allpowerful 'they', exerts the pressures of conformity. Individuals must have jobs, they must perform functions the end-product of which is the smooth running of society itself. There is no place for those without a *function*.

1. Das Furchtbare ist, daß ich keinen Beruf habe. Man muß ja jetzt einen Beruf haben. Sie sagen es . . . sie sagen, man ist faul, wenn man keinen Beruf hat. (*Wanderer, kommst du nach Spa . . .* p. 131)

> The dreadful thing is that I have no job. You have to have a job now. They say so . . . they say you're lazy if you haven't got a job.

The individual feels himself constantly threatened by the anonymous power of the state and is just as helpless and afraid as he was when caught up in the war. Jupp *Der Mann mit den Messern* says of his audience:

> 2. . . . denn sie haben alle immer Angst. Sie schleppen die Angst hinter sich wie einen schweren Schatten . . . (Ibid., p. 19)
>
>> . . . for they are always afraid. They drag their fear behind them like a dense shadow . . .

The faceless society with its endless resources has the power to give and to withhold. All the individual can do is to wait and hope like the young man at the station in the story *An der Angel*.

> 3. . . . diese Clique hat Kraft und Sicherheit, während wir— wir Wartenden, wir haben nichts; wir leben auf des Messers Schneide, wir balancieren uns von einer Minute der Hoffnung zur anderen Minute der Hoffnung. (Ibid., p. 136)
>
>> . . . this clique has power and security whilst we—we who wait, we have nothing, we live on the knife's edge, we balance from one minute of hope to the next.

'They' hold the key to hope and despair, to light and darkness and they use their power quite arbitrarily. We are deceived and driven to despair. We are on the hook.

> 4. Sie halten uns an der Angel, immer wieder beißen wir an, immer wieder lassen wir uns hochziehen bis an die Oberfläche, immer wieder atmen wir eine Minute das Licht, die Schönheit, die Freude, und immer wieder lacht so ein Schwein, läßt die Schnur locker, und wir sitzen im Dunkeln . . . (Ibid., p. 137)

> They keep us on the hook, again and again we bite, again and again,
> they haul us up to the surface, we breathe light, beauty, joy, again
> and again some pig laughs, lets the line go slack and we are left in
> darkness . . .

Society is monstrous just as war was monstrous, *using, exploiting* and *consuming* the individual; it is like Jupp's audience, a crouching animal before whom he waits helpless and afraid.

> 5. . . . vor diesem flimmernden, lüsternen, vieltausendköp-
>   figen, gespannten Ungeheuer, das im Finstern wie zum
>   Sprung da saß . . . (Ibid., p. 24)

>> . . . before this tense, flickering, greedy, hydra-headed monster,
>> sitting in the darkness ready to spring . . .

(b) THE INDIVIDUAL

In such a society, how is the individual to react? During the war he was controlled and deployed; as a civilian he finds himself manipulated and exploited. Either he *conforms* and is willing to perform the role allotted to him or he *protests* and is cast out as the misfit, the outsider.

1. The Conformists

These are the people who have quickly found their feet, individuals from whom war has not demanded too high a price. They slide back into position and click into place. They adapt to post-war society and quickly take on the colour and shape prescribed for them. Slick and self-confident they get off the tram.

> 1. Und als wir nach Hause kamen, sind sie aus dem Krieg
>   ausgestiegen wie aus einer Straßenbahn, die gerade dort
>   etwas langsamer fuhr, wo sie wohnten, sie sind abgesprun-
>   gen, ohne den Fahrpreis zu bezahlen . . .; man umarmte

sie . . . and am nächsten Morgen ging man fragen, ob die
Stelle noch frei war: die Stelle war noch frei. Es war alles
tadellos, die Krankenkasse lief weiter, man ließ sich ein
bißchen entnazifizieren—so wie man zum Friseur geht,
um den lästigen Bart abzunehmen zu lassen— (*Wanderer,
kommst du nach Spa . . .* p. 133)

> And when we came home, they got out of the war like getting off a
> tram, which slowed down exactly where they lived, they jumped off
> without paying the fare . . . they were welcomed lovingly . . . and
> the next day they went to ask if their job was still open: it was.
> Everything was perfect, sickness benefit was still being paid, they
> underwent a little denazification just like going to the barbers to
> get rid of a tiresome beard.

These are the ones who have adapted. Whatever society
demands of them, they are willing to become. Bur-Malottke,
Doktor Murkes gesammeltes Schweigen, changes his beliefs to fit
the current vogue. He was converted in the general religious
enthusiasm of 1945 and later, when this becomes unfashionable,
reverts to his original attitudes. Integrity is a meaningless word,
particularly in the business world where the real predators of
the social jungle roam, and which frequently bears the brunt of
Böll's contempt. Relationships are cultivated with a view to
their usefulness. Compromises and concessions are made, deals
are completed, advantage is carefully weighed. Success and
genuine human relationships seem mutually exclusive. The
well-trained young wife in the story *Wie in schlechten Romanen*
skilfully manipulates her husband's first business deal but at
a cost to their marriage.

> 2. Ich blickte auf Berthas kleine bräunliche Hände, mit
> denen sie sicher und ruhig steuerte. Hände, dachte ich, die
> Schecks unterschreiben und auf Mayonnaisetuben drück-
> en, und ich blickte höher- auf ihren Mund und spürte auch
> jetzt keine Lust, ihn zu küssen. (*Als der Krieg ausbrach*,
> p. 121)

I looked at Bertha's small tanned hands with which she drove so
calmly and safely. Hands, I thought, which sign cheques, press tubes
of mayonnaise, and I raised my eyes to her mouth and even now felt
no desire to kiss it.

Business ethics appertain at all levels. The former black-
marketeer, *Geschäft ist Geschäft*, who has become legitimate
and has his own stall, has done so at the expense of his humanity. Once he had given away cigarettes and talked of old times,
but now he chooses not to recognize his former friend and
drives away a small girl who has not quite enough money for
sweets. Playing the social game corrupts. The conformist
conforms at the expense of human relationships.

2. The Non-conformists

These are of two types:

(*a*) Those who have been so shaken by the war that they are
unable to come to terms with society: *the drop-outs*.

(*b*) Those who are able to stand outside and observe society
and are then *unwilling* to live on its terms: *the opt-outs*.

Type (*a*)

He is the individual who has not been agile enough to leap from
the tram at the right time, too burdened by his experiences and
his feeling of inferiority to make the decision and risk its
consequences.

1. Wir aber fuhren inzwischen weiter mit der Straßenbahn
   und warteten, ob irgendwo eine Station käme, die uns
   bekannt genug vorgekommen wäre, daß wir auszusteigen
   riskiert hätten: die Haltestelle kam nicht . . . Wir aber
   fuhren weiter und weiter, der Fahrpreis erhöhte sich auto-
   matisch, und wir hatten außerdem für grosses und

schweres Gepäck den Preis zu entrichten: für die
bleierne Masse des Nichts, die wir mitzuschleppen hatten
. . . aber die Endstation kam nicht . . . (*Wanderer, kommst
du nach Spa . . .*, pp. 133–4)

Meanwhile we stayed on the tram and waited to see whether any stop
was familiar enough to let us risk getting off. The stop did not come
. . . we went on and on, the fare rose automatically and we had to
find the fare for the big heavy kit bag: for the leaden weight of point-
lessness which we dragged with us . . . but the terminus never came.

Those who cannot conform, whose nerves have gone, who
cannot dismiss the war but still bear along with them the
awareness of the nothingness of existence, are looked on with
suspicion by the faceless beings in whose hands their fate lies
(*die Kontrolleure*). They are a highly suspicious lot (*eine
äusserst verdächtige Sippschaft*), totally inadequate since their
sense of nothingness extends to themselves.

2. „Sie sind?" . . . sagte sie.
„Nichts," sagte ich, „absolut nichts. Sehen Sie mich als
einen Vetreter des Nichts an . . ." (Ibid., p. 58)

'You are?' . . . she said.
'Nothing,' I said, 'absolutely nothing. Look upon me as a representative of nothingness . . .'

In a bright and busy society—Wundsiedel's factory with its
bright buildings and busy people—there is no place for the
troubled, the anxious, the indifferent. Indifference is the hall-
mark of this type of non-conformist.

3. Es war mir jetzt alles egal . . ., (Ibid., p. 133)

4. Im Grunde genommen ist mir egal, was sie denken.
(Ibid., p. 131)

5. Mir ist alles gleich . . . mir war alles gleichgültig. (Ibid., p. 23)

6. Mir war alles scheißegal . . . (Ibid., p. 24)

> Now it was all the same to me . . .
>
> I don't really care what they think.
>
> I was indifferent about everything . . .
>
> I couldn't have cared less . . .

Inactivity. These individuals cannot find work and therefore are an anathema to a society in which activity *per se* is the supreme virtue. The job they do find, the shifting of rubble, binds them more closely to their experience of total destruction. It seems to them senseless to work. They contemplate the countless number of days it takes to build a bridge or a house and the seconds it takes to blow them to bits.

1. Wozu da noch arbeiten? Ich finde es sinnlos, da noch zu arbeiten. Ich glaube, das ist es, was mich verrückt macht . . . (*Wanderer, kommst du nach Spa . . .* p. 131)

> Why work? I find it stupid to go on working. I think that's what drives me mad . . .

They drop out. They leave society to get on without them. They are casual workers, working only to provide themselves with bread, a few cigarettes, a drink. For the most part they accept their lot. They lie on the bed, smoke and dream.

2. Am liebsten liege ich auf dem Bett und träume. (Ibid., p. 131)

3. Ich mietete ein Zimmer in der Stadt, dort lag ich auf dem Bett, rauchte und wartete und wußte nicht, worauf ich wartete. Arbeiten zu gehen, hatte ich keine Lust. (*Als der Krieg ausbrach*, p. 134)

4. Ich hatte . . . einen Beruf, wo ich mich nur hinzustellen
   brauchte und ein bißchen zu träumen. (*Wanderer, kommst
   du nach Spa* . . . p. 26)

> I liked best to lie on my bed and dream.
>
> I rented a room in town. There I lay on the bed, smoked and waited
> and did not know what I was waiting for. I had no desire to work.
>
> I had a job where I need only stand there and dream a little.

Type (b)

It is this characteristic of not engaging in the rat race, of using
time to consider and observe rather than to participate, which
is common to both types of social drop-out. It is basic to the
deliberate non-conformist. He provides the antidote to the men
of the opportunist society *ohne Erinnerungsvermögen, die
nicht rückwärts blicken*[1] who look upon *Nachdenken*[1] as morbid
introspection. The ability *to remember, to observe* and *to think*
are the qualities of Böll's endearing black sheep of society *die
schwarzen Schafe*. They are quite able to meet society on its
terms, to follow the pattern, but are aware of the trap and refuse
to be caught in it. They know it is a matter of life and death.

The narrator in *Es wird etwas geschehen* describes the 'black
sheep' disposition in this way:

1. Von Natur bin ich mehr dem Nachdenken und dem
   Nichtstun zugeneigt als der Arbeit . . . (*Nicht nur zur
   Weihnachtszeit*, p. 81)

> By nature I am more inclined to thinking things out and doing
> nothing than to work . . .

Dreaming, doing nothing, are common characteristics to both
types of non-conformists but here the resemblance ends. Those

---

[1] cf. p. 34, Quote 6.

in the second category are more than capable of getting to grips with society. *They opt out*. Obtaining a post in Wunsiedel's factory is child's play; the narrator passes his tests with ease. He knows how society thinks and is always several moves ahead. Like Doktor Murke, he is highly efficient but he is never taken in. He finally finds his ideal vocation, improbably enough, as professional mourner at funerals, an occupation in which pensiveness and doing nothing are primary qualifications.

Those who do not conform by choice are happy because they have found the *freedom* to live their own lives. They are the only free ones in a society that seeks to bind and limit. They are natural Bohemians.

> 2. . . . ich badete mich im Air der Ungepflegtheit und trank zum Frühstück, trank mittags und abends den Honigseim der Bohème: das tiefe Glücksgefühl, mit der Gesellschaft nicht konform zu sein. (Ibid., p. 123)

> . . . I immersed myself in an air of general neglect and drank for breakfast, mid-day and at night the nectar of the Bohemian: that feeling of intense happiness which comes from not conforming to society.

They are the sharp-eyed. Their vision is unrestricted in a society blinkered by success and material prosperity. They are the ones who are aware of what is going wrong. Franz, *Nicht nur zur Weihnachtszeit*, has refused to follow the traditional path into the family business. He lives his own life, estranged from his family. Yet he is the only one to see the dangerous situation into which his family, by their humouring of Tante Milla, has been led. Because of his position as 'Black Sheep' no one will listen.

> 3. Doch . . . besaß er zu wenig Reputation, um in der Verwandtschaft Gehör zu finden. (Ibid., p. 8)

> He had too little reputation to warrant being heard by his relatives.

Franz makes his protest but is disregarded. The non-conformist is the protestor and *in him lies all hope of social change*. This is the paradox of the situation. Society sees in him its natural enemy and protects itself by ignoring him, by casting him out and so perpetuates itself without the leavening he could bring. He is forced into hiding, compelled to withdraw into an inner life, to protect his secret freedom. He applies for a job in the factory, gives the required answers to the questions, pretends to believe in accepted procedure, *Es muß etwas geschehen*. He acts his part so well that his employers think he has their interests at heart, *Die Postkarte*

> 4. Denn man ist überzeugt, daß ich an der Firma hänge und etwas für sie tun werde. Aber ich hänge nicht an ihr und denke nicht daran, etwas für sie zu tun . . . (*Als der Krieg ausbrach*, p. 85)

> For people are convinced that I live for the firm and will do great things for it. But I am not devoted to it and do not intend to do anything for it . . .

Doktor Murke performs his job most efficiently and makes only a *private* protest by collecting his silences and sticking the garish religious picture on the elegant door. The man who has studied at five universities and has gained two doctorates withdraws to be an announcer at a railway station, finding satisfaction in his *private* knowledge that the revered objects he extolls are fakes, *Hier ist Tibten*. The man on the bridge omits his girl-friend from the statistics for his *private* satisfaction, *An der Brücke*.

In their various ways the non-conformists protest against society and in this way retain their freedom and preserve their integrity. They do not compromise with themselves and yet in the private nature of their protests lies a kind of compromise with society. They preserve their integrity at the cost of *with-*

drawal, disguise, play-acting. Stretching out his arms Jupp, *Der Mann mit den Messern,* has moments when he is transported to another world where other laws are valid and from them he draws the strength to live his life and despise his audience.

5. Auf seinem nüchternen Gesicht erschien etwas seltsam Kühl-Träumerisches, etwas halb Besessenes und halb Kaltes, Magisches, das mich maßlos erschreckte. ,,So,'' sagte er leise, ,,ich greife einfach hinein in die Atmosphäre, und ich spüre, wie meine Hände länger und länger werden und wie sie hinaufgreifen in einen Raum, in dem andere Gesetze gültig sind, sie stoßen durch eine Decke, und dort oben liegen seltsame, bezaubernde Spannungen, die ich greife, . . .'' (*Wanderer, kommst du nach Spa . . .* p. 21)

On his sober face there appeared something strangely remote and dreamlike, something half possessed yet half cold, something magical, which horrified me . . . 'There,' he said softly, 'I simply reach out into the atmosphere and I feel my hands grow longer and longer, reaching out into a place where other laws apply, they push their way through a covering and up there, there are strange magical forces which I take hold of . . . .

The non-conformists have their own world from which they draw their strength and from which they can *despise* society. The dilemma facing Böll in many of his stories is to find a way whereby those with vision *do not withdraw* but confront society and *actively contribute* to its reform. The step from not conforming to active participation in the reforming of society is a problem that preoccupies Böll in his longer fictional works.

(*c*) THE ALIEN WORLD

War is a monster; society is a monster; but always in Böll it is *the external world itself which is the real enemy* and in their

treatment of the individual, war and society are only manifestations of the essential otherness, of what appears as objective reality in which the individual struggles to find his place.
In war, the individual was just a number in a regiment; in
society, just a statistic, just a cog; in the external world he is
just another *unrelated object*.

The individual as a member of society contributes to his own
insecurity by playing into the hands of this watching, waiting
world. Society, apparently in league with it, has robbed itself
of all meaning, has made a fetish of dehumanization and this
image Böll projects in the satires. It is a world of statistics, of
ceaseless, meaningless activity, perpetuating itself as a planned
and organized function. It is ridiculous, grotesque and frighteningly credible.

The man on the bridge counts those who cross over it and
the statisticians pounce on his figures. Enthusiastically they
reduce people to numbers on a sheet where they can handle
them, formulate them and spin endless combinations, draw
endless conclusions for a remote future.

1. Und dann fangen sie an zu multiplizieren, zu dividieren,
   zu prozentualisieren, ich weiß nicht was. Sie rechnen aus,
   wieviel heute jede Minute über die Brücke gehen und
   wieviel in zehn Jahren über die Brücke gegangen sein
   werden. (*Wanderer, kommst du nach Spa* . . . p. 62)

   And then they begin to multiply, to divide, to percentage and heaven
   knows what. They work out how much traffic crosses the bridge each
   minute and how much will have crossed the bridge in ten years.

The walls of the man who throws things away for a living,
Der Wegwerfer, are hung with graphs and charts. He is
engaged in the negative task of throwing away unwanted information that comes through the post. He is the embodiment

of an absurd, yet in the world as it exists, a necessary activity. Three sacks of mail are reduced to one small packet before it reaches its destination. The perpetual arrival of this extraneous material, his own collection of it as a child investigating his father's waste-paper basket, underlines the situation in which the individual finds himself the object of a perpetual bombardment of unrelated material, of detailed yet unconnected information conjuring up an external world of senseless chaos. Even more alarming is the scientific investigation *der Wegwerfer* makes into this situation. With stopwatch and paper he calculates the tremendous wastage of time in the production and unwrapping of this material. He carries out a systematic time and motion study of the senseless and engages in a wild fantasy that is pushed to the edge of madness. The point of departure into the absurd is when the colossal wastage of energy is accepted and a scientific approach is made to solve *the result* instead of attacking *the source*. He does not question the production of useless things but sets up a complicated system to deal with it. Society accuses him of nihilism and yet he is the one who has thought things out to their logical conclusion. *He has seen into the absurdity of the world itself.*[1]

The frenzied activity of society is part of the defence mechanism. Provided individuals are kept busy and prevented from thinking things out to their inevitable conclusion, there is some hope of keeping the menacing world at bay. If time and space are filled apparently purposefully the empty void will not be noticed. Wunsiedel's factory is full of busy people to whom activity is life. Producing and organizing are of primary importance. What is actually manufactured there is mentioned only as an afterthought at the end of the story. Smooth functioning will give the impression that all is in order. The futility of this approach is shown repeatedly in the satires. Wunsiedel dies, activity comes to an abrupt end and in the appalled

---

[1] cf. Jeziorkowski: *Rhythmus und Figur*. A stimulating analysis of this aspect of Böll's work and of the theme of alienation.

silence that follows, the sinister stirring of the predatory alien world is heard. The wild laughter of despair rings out.

2. . . . plötzlich traf uns eine Welle wilden Lachens . . . so stark, daß ich erschrak . . . (Ibid., pp. 22–3)

> . . . suddenly a wave of wild laughter broke over us . . . so powerful that I was afraid . . .

It is the laughter that sounds in the dreams of the *Wegwerfer* as he is pursued by his formulae, his endless calculations; the laughter of the general *Hauptstädtisches Journal* surrounded by thousands of statues of himself.

3. . . . manche Formeln explodieren wie Dynamit, das Geräusch der Explosion klingt wie ein großes Lachen: es ist mein eigenes . . . (*Nicht nur zur Weihnachtszeit*, p. 133)

> . . . many formulae explode like dynamite, the noise of the explosion sounds like a huge burst of laughter: it is my own . . .

4. Ich lachte, und tausendfach kam das Lachen aus meinem eigenen Munde auf mich zurück. (Ibid., p. 113)

> I laughed and my laugh echoed about me a thousandfold from my own mouth.

To sum up: the satires reinforce the earlier themes of individual violation, exploitation and alienation, but they express less confidence that a solution is feasible. In spite of the laughter we are conscious of Böll's growing despair. We feel the conflict between his *intellectual awareness*: that individual freedom lies in *withdrawal* and opting out and his *moral conviction*: that it is to be found in *participation* and in the service of others.

4

The Novels

In this title the word Novel is used to cover all the longer narrative works of Böll although they differ in length and form. A similar development can be traced in these longer works to that in the short story. The approach gradually shifts from immediate passionate involvement to an ironic detachment. No attempt has been made to give a comprehensive analysis of each work—that lies outside the scope of this book—but those elements in form and content which contribute to the major issues of concern to Böll have been noted under the following headings:

A. Time: The Key to Form.
B. Social Comment.
C. Withdrawal.
D. Participation.

A. Time:[1] The Key to Form

The thesis that the German past is dead, separated from the present by an unbridgeable gap, that one can nevertheless not forget it but must come to terms, that it is vital to recognize what is real and valid, makes Böll's confrontation with time an issue of major importance and eventually dictates the form and technique of the novels.

Der Zug war pünktlich (1949) and *Wo warst du, Adam?* (1951) both in conception and setting parallel the early short stories.

[1] cf. Reid, *Time in the Works of Heinrich Böll*, for a detailed analysis of this aspect.

They embody Böll's search for a new form of expression while
his mind is still obsessed by the short story technique—the
relating of a single encounter with life. The former is best
described as an *Erzählung* since it is in effect an extended short
story; the latter is more a collection of short stories, each
chapter showing a different face of war and virtually self-
contained. With their completion Böll is able to free himself of
war as a theme, and to break through the short story barrier.
The theme of war demands an episodic approach because it is
the *fragmentation of experience* into senseless, unrelated
episodes. The demands of the post-war world are for *integra-
tion*, for *meaning*, for *cohesion*. Böll asks that the more engaged
a writer is, the better he should write, that is, the more his work
in form and content should reflect the needs of the contemporary world. Later novels give evidence of Böll's adapting
his style of writing to the contemporary need.

(*a*) THE OPPRESSIVE PAST

In the next two novels *Und sagte kein einziges Wort* (1953) and
Haus ohne Hüter (1954) Böll's technique begins to evolve. Set
in the present, September 1952, and autumn 1953 respectively,
they are concerned with people desperately in need of integra-
tion. Exhausted by the past Fred Bogner is unable to take the
present seriously. He can find no meaning in what has happened
to him and consequently nothing in his present is valid. His is
the

1. . . . Gesicht eines Mannes, der zu früh von Gleichgültig-
keit erfaßt wurde gegen alles, was ernst zu nehmen andere
Männer sich entschlossen haben. (*Und sagte kein einziges
Wort*, p. 39)

. . . face of a man touched too early by indifference towards all those
things other men have decided to treat seriously.

The only thing about which he has no doubts is death.

    2. . . . die einzige Wahrheit, an der mir nie Zweifel kommt.
       (Ibid., p. 85)

       . . . the one fact I never doubt.

Nella, Frau Brielach, even Albert, are in their different ways
imprisoned in the past and unable to live a satisfactory life in
the present. Between past and present an extra dimension is
inserted: the time that never was but might have been, *die
dritte Ebene*, the third level.

    3. . . . die Zeit, die nie gewesen, das Leben, das nie gelebt
       worden war . . . (*Haus ohne Hüter*, p. 74)

       . . . the time that had never been, the life that had never been
       lived . . .

    4. . . . er verfiel in Nellas Krankheit, sich auf die dritte
       Ebene zu begeben . . . (Ibid., p. 97)

       . . . he had caught Nella's disease of retreating to the third level of
       existence . . .

    5. . . . er hatte wieder angefangen, auf der dritten Ebene zu
       leben . . . (Ibid., p. 147)

       . . . he had started living on the third level again . . .

From their position in the present, by means of flashback and
interior monologue they slip into the past, into the future that
might have been, until chronological time loses all meaning.

(b) TIMELESSNESS

In *Das Brot der frühen Jahre* (1955) *Billard um halb zehn* (1959) and *Ansichten eines Clowns* (1963) the further device of concentration, together with a more involved use of symbol and *leitmotif* is added to this technique. The events in the first novel, which range over Walter's adolescence and early manhood, are compressed into one day.

> 1. Der Tag, an dem Hedwig kam, war ein Montag . . . (*Das Brot der frühen Jahre*, p. 5)

> The day on which Hedwig arrived was a Monday . . .

It is Monday morning, 15 March; the date is specific, events are carefully chronicled and minutely observed but the narrative is so thick with symbol and past and present are so tightly interwoven and so skilfully presented that we too can scarcely realize that it is still Monday.

> 2. Es war halb acht, und es schien mir, die Ewigkeit müßte ein Montag sein: es war noch nicht elf Stunden her, seit ich das Haus verlassen hatte. (Ibid., p. 144)

> It was half past seven and it seemed to me eternity must be a Monday. It was not yet eleven hours since I had left home.

In *Billard um halb zehn* one day, 6 September 1958, becomes the focal point of fifty years. Again events are keyed to specific dates and are placed clearly in time. The hours, even the seconds, are noted as Johanna listens on the telephone to the speaking clock, but the layers of time glide smoothly over one another and one is left suspended in timelessness. Hugo listens to the words of Robert Fähmel

3. . . . die ihn sechzig Jahre zurück, zwanzig vor, wieder
zehn zurück und plötzlich in die Wirklichkeit des Kalen-
derblatts draußen warfen . . . (*Billard um halb zehn*,
p. 43)

> . . . which catapulted him sixty years back, twenty forwards yet
> again ten years back and suddenly into the reality of the actual date
> on the calendar . . .

The same basic material is presented from different stand-
points in time. Actions are repeated in time and place as memories are evoked by different characters. Time is defined yet
elusive as it shifts from past to present; places are described in
detail and yet change as they are seen through different eyes;
characters are equally insubstantial as they assume the identities
given to them by others. The repetition of symbols makes us
recall and associate all previous occurrences when that symbol
was used. In this way past and present are simultaneously
present in the mind. The technique is applied strikingly in
Ansichten eines Clowns where Schnier's life is compressed into
an hour or two and practically the whole novel is one interior
monologue. The time in Schnier's flat is timeless. He, and we,
are suspended in eternity.

(*c*) THE MOMENT

With the arrival of Hedwig the foundations of Walter Fendrich's life shift and the day achieves a timeless quality. It is a
happening without parallel when a human consciousness is for
a moment in contact with reality. Heinrich Brielach *Haus ohne
Hüter* witnesses just such a rare moment. He catches the
fleeting look in his mother's eyes when she realizes communication and love are still possible. He observes the sudden awareness that lasts for a fraction of a second (*Tausendstelsekunde
der überraschenden Erkenntnis*).

1. . . . nur *für einen Augenblick*, aber er wußte, daß *ein Augenblick* viel ist. (*Haus ohne Hüter*, p. 220)

> . . . *just for a moment*, but he knew that *a moment* is a great deal.

Walter experiences a similar liberating moment as he follows Hedwig from the station and it is enough to change the preconceptions on which his life has till then been built. It is sufficient to dissolve all previous time, to discard it like a shrunken shirt.

2. . . . und ich dachte wieder an Ulla und an die Jahre mit ihr: diese Jahre waren eng geworden, wie ein Hemd, das die Wäsche nicht überstanden hat—die Zeit aber seit Mittag . . . war eine andere Zeit. (*Das Brot der frühen Jahre*, p. 143)

> . . . and I thought of Ulla again and of the years spent with her, these years had shrunk like a shirt that had not stood up to washing—the time since noon was a different time.

In such significant moments reality is to be found. Hans Schnier is a clown and observes such moments in order to capture the essence of reality.

3. „Ich bin ein Clown," sagte ich, „und sammle Augenblicke." (*Ansichten eines Clowns*, p. 246)

> 'I am a clown,' I said, 'and I collect moments.'

These moments are rare and unpredictable. We must be alert, we must guard against the dulling action of routine or we will miss reality altogether; we may never begin to live.

4. Später dachte ich oft darüber nach, wie alles gekommen wäre, wenn ich Hedwig nicht am Bahnhof abgeholt hätte:

ich wäre in ein anderes Leben eingestiegen, wie man aus
Versehen in einen anderen Zug steigt . . . (*Das Brot der
frühen Jahre*, p. 6)

> Later I often thought about how things would have been if I had not
> met Hedwig at the station. I would have got into another life as one
> gets into another train, by mistake . . .

Yet the moment is by its very nature transient and Schnier
warns against trying to perpetuate or repeat it. One cannot even
share it for to each one it is something different.

5. Man soll Augenblicke lassen, nie wiederholen. (*Ansichten
   eines Clowns*, p. 209)

   > One should leave moments alone, never repeat them.

6. Man kann Augenblicke nicht wiederholen und nicht
   mitteilen. (Ibid., p. 209)

   > One cannot repeat moments nor communicate them.

The form of Böll's novels is all important. His conception of
the nature of time is fundamental to his view of the nature of
reality. Stretches of time *die routinierte Zeit*, are unimpor-
tant: *die Aktualität*. Meaningful only are those moments
of illumination when the individual glimpses reality: *die
Wirklichkeit*. Then *being* suddenly *makes sense* and *existence* is
transformed into *life*.

B. Social Comment

In the novels with their wider scope Böll is able to give his
readers a comprehensive view of the acquisitive materialistic
society. The short stories pinpoint isolated criticism: social

injustice,[1] business ethics,[2] militarism.[3] The larger field of the major work provides room to illustrate the complicity of State, Church and Army, the complexity of their involvement in the preservation of the status quo and the extent of their guilt in the creation of the inhumane society. Because of this involvement it becomes politic in all spheres

> 1. . . . sich mit den Mächtigen dieser Welt zu arrangieren . . . (*Ende einer Dienstfahrt* p. 98)

> . . . to accommodate oneself to the strong of this world . . .

(*a*) BÜFFEL AND LÄMMER

Society is divided into the strong and the weak, the rich and the poor, the manipulators and the manipulated. Böll illustrates this by his symbolism of *Büffel und Lämmer*. He speaks of the *Sakrament des Büffels* and the *Sakrament des Lammes*.

> 1. „Wir sind Lämmer . . . haben geschworen' nie vom *Sakrament des Büffels* zu essen." (*Billard um halb zehn*, p. 39)

> 'We are lambs . . . we have sworn never to eat of the sacrament of the buffalo.'

> 2. . . . ich sehnte mich nach dem weißen, leichten Sakrament des Lammes . . . (Ibid., p. 127)

> . . . I longed for the white, light sacrament of the lamb . . .

To eat of the sacrament of the buffalo is *to conform* to the materialistic society and accept its values: to eat of the sacra-

---

[1] *Die Waage der Baleks.*
[2] *Wie in schlechten Romanen.*
[3] *Hauptstädtisches Journal.*

ment of the lamb is *to secede* from that society, aware of its shallow pretension. The choice is there for each individual but the temptation to taste of the wrong sacrament is great since its rewards are considerable and immediate. A taste suffices to corrupt for ever. Those who acquire such a taste take on the brute strength, the formidable tenacity, the insensitivity and the herd instinct characteristic of the buffalo. Those who refrain, preserve the innocence, guilelessness and gentleness of the sacrificial lamb. The *Büffel* are the opportunists, the short-sighted materialists who see no further than immediate self-interest: the *Lämmer* are the non-conformists, the selfless visionaries who become the unprotesting victims of the predatory society. In *Billard um halb zehn* Nettlinger and Schrella epitomize the two types, but they are found throughout the novels. The *Büffel* invariably function successfully in the Army, in politics, in the Church. The *Lämmer* never think in terms of self-advancement or self-preservation. They devote themselves to the service of others, resisting passively the onslaught of the materialistic society.

Insensitivity towards everything outside the area of self-interest marks the *Büffel* in all spheres. Self-assured, Nettlinger offers a bribe to Jochen; the politicians in the Hotel Prinz Heinrich decide on their vote-catching policies without regard for what is needed; the General obsessed with the idea of an unimpeded firing range, does not care what lies between him and his object; Oberst Bressen shouts about counter-attacks to his sickened, exhausted men; the aesthetic Catholics enthuse about their literary circles and disregard their Christian duties. This is particularly true of the Bishop *Und sagte kein einziges Wort* who incorporates in himself elements of Church, Army and social élite. He has held high office in the Army, now holds a similar high position in the Church and enjoys the ensuing privileges his friendship with the wealthy foreigner brings, to whose home and library he has access. Revelling in his public procession, pursuing his private academic interests, believing he has no needs since they are all met, he is quite insensitive to the needs of others. Like Leo, Schnier's brother:

3. Er war nicht bedürfnislos wie Franz von Assisi, der sich die Bedürfnisse anderer Menschen vorstellen konnte, ohwohl er selbst auch bedürfnislos war. (*Ansichten eines Clowns*, p. 205)

> He was not free from desire in the way Francis of Assisi was, who could imagine that others might have desires and needs, although he himself did not.

The Bishop has an ascetic face, highly suited to reproduction in religious magazines. The Church is influenced by an imposing presence and intellectual pretensions and these take precedence over genuine sincerity, if this is embodied in an unprepossessing individual. The stolid, conscientious priest of peasant stock is a non-starter in competition with ambitious young priests with photogenic faces like advertisements for skin preparations. These are the opportunist career priests, smug and elegant.

4. Hier . . . in meiner Kirche werden die Messen der durchreisenden Priester gelesen, sie kommen aus den umliegenden Hotels, gepflegte Männer, die zu Tagungen fahren, von Tagungen kommen . . . die den Geruch exquisiter Hotelbadezimmer in meiner verfallenen Sakristei hinterlassen. (*Und sagte kein einziges Wort*, p. 75)

> Here in my church mass is read by visiting priests, coming from nearby hotels, well-groomed men, travelling to conferences, back from conferences, bringing with them the perfume of exquisite hotel bathrooms into my tumbledown sacristy.

The pomp and ceremony of the Bishop's procession shows clearly that the social structure of the church is as fixed as that of the society with which it is in league. Each has his place and is accepted or ignored accordingly. Those who profess to be intellectual and who look the part are preferred to those who humbly serve.

(b) INHUMANITY

Insensitivity leads to inhumanity; because Church and society are insensitive to individual human need, human contact has been lost and both have become inhumane. Symptomatic of this is the attitude to *wealth*. Poverty pervades the life of the Bogner family on such a scale and over such a period of time that it is like a disease, an invisible dust lodging in the lungs. Lack of sufficient money to live distorts the life of Heinrich Brielach. Böll contrasts this with the enormous wealth of the Church, of the drug companies, of Hans Schnier's father. On this scale money ceases to be a means to an end: the provision of food, housing, warmth for human beings. It is *abstract* wealth, figures in accounts, shares to be manipulated, used only to amass more abstract money.

> 1. . . . nicht das konkrete, mit dem man Milch kauft und Taxi fährt . . . und ins Kino geht—nur das abstrakte . . . er konnte sein Geld nicht einem Clown geben, der mit Geld nur eins tun würde: es ausgeben, genau das Gegenteil von dem, was man mit Geld tun mußte. (*Ansichten eines Clowns*, pp. 175–6)

> > . . . not concrete wealth, with which one buys milk or pays for a taxi and goes to the cinema, but abstract wealth . . . he could not give his money to a clown who would do only one thing with it: spend it, precisely the opposite of what one should do with money.

Between humanity and society is an invisible wall:

> 2. . . . wo das Geld aufhörte, zum Ausgeben da zu sein, wo es unantastbar wurde und in Tabernakeln als Ziffer existierte. (Ibid., p. 176)

> > . . . where money ceased to be for spending where it became untouchable and existed only as figures.

There is a similar barrier in the Catholic community between organizational activities and Christian duty, concern for cultural abstractions and awareness of individual welfare. All too frequently the social reject is the outcast of the Church, too. Frau Franke is both a respected member of the Church and the Bogner's landlady, the prototype of the conscientious Catholic who fulfils to the letter all the organizational duties placed upon her by the Church but has neither sympathy nor understanding for her tenants. She places the abstract above the real, piety above love and pity. Similarly the Catholic circle in Bonn, *Ansichten eines Clowns*, an intellectual group which meets to combine interest in cultural subjects with prayer, discusses academically the relativity of the conception of poverty, and complacently tells stories to illustrate how witty, understanding and broad-minded modern Catholics are. If the Church confines itself to organization and discussion and forgets its practical Christian action it becomes as abstract as wealth that remains unused.

(*c*) MATERIALISM

The arid emptiness of the materialistic society is exposed by Böll in *Das Brot der frühen Jahre*. Walter Fendrich, deprived in his early life, has not resigned himself like Fred Bogner. He has become an electrician, has acquired a technical skill suited to a soulless society, and has reaped material benefit.

1. Ich hatte mich zurechtgefunden . . . Es ist alles ganz passabel. (*Das Brot der frühen Jahre*, pp. 32–3)

   I had found my feet . . . Things are not so bad.

Yet he has not completely sold out. Although cynically prepared to accept what society offers, he is still wary. This gives him the ability to stand outside himself and see what he has become.

2. . . . ich spürte, daß etwas Wölfisches in mir war. (Ibid., p. 20)

3. . . . niemand schien etwas zu wissen, etwas zu spüren von dem Wolf, der in mir hauste. (Ibid., p. 24)

. . . I felt there was something of the wolf in me.

. . . no one seemed to suspect it.

He sees himself growing rapacious, cunning and as insatiable as his fellows. He is like them. He has conformed to their ways. With the revelation of Hedwig, awareness becomes certainty and he knows he must escape from Ulla, to whom employees are numbers or names in a ledger to be neatly scored out when they die; he must escape from an economic miracle where the individual is a thing to be exploited and discarded, from a society in which humaneness is an unknown word.

(d) THE HUMANE SOCIETY

Shortly after this literary confrontation with the new society Böll wrote *Irisches Tagebuch*, his Irish diary

1. Als ich an Bord des Dampfers ging, sah ich, hörte und roch ich, daß ich eine Grenze überschritten hatte . . . (*Irisches Tagebuch*, p. 7)

When I boarded the steamer my senses told me that I had crossed a frontier . . .

In going to Ireland Böll felt he had crossed a frontier in more than a physical sense. He felt he had entered another world with different values, a different social order.

2. . . . hier schon nahm Europas soziale Ordnung andere Formen an. (Ibid., p. 7)

. . . here Europe has developed a different kind of social organization.

Ireland is *Europas glühendes Herz*, the *warm* heart of Europe, a country where poverty is no cause for shame or material success the focus of unreserved admiration. The Irish seem free from the social and economic pressures that bedevil other countries. In Ireland there is room to develop and time to reflect, unharried by the ceaseless activity of the self-important assertion of modern society, the senseless preoccupation with superficial aims. The diary is not an idyll. Böll is aware of the high price Ireland pays for its failure to adjust to modern life. But he senses in Ireland what is lacking in prosperous Europe, in the materialistic society he has rejected through Walter Fendrich.

> 3. . . . ein solches Land bietet die Chance des Humanen . . .
> (Wolfdietrich Rasch: *In Sachen Böll*, p. 265)

> . . . such a country offers a chance for humane behaviour . .

Such a society offers time and opportunity for individual growth, for human contact, for communication, for the manifestation of human love. It gives humanity the chance to be humane.

C. Withdrawal

> 1. Es wird dringend zur Entfernung von der Truppe geraten. Zur Fahnenflucht und Desertion wird eher zu—als von ihr abgeraten . . . (*Als der Krieg ausbrach*, p. 260)

> I sincerely urge you to go absent without leave. You are advised to desert the colours, you are warned not to stay.

> 2. Daß Menschenwerdung dann beginnt, wenn einer sich von der jeweiligen Truppe entfernt, diese Erfahrung gebe

ich hier unumwunden als Ratschlag an spätere Geschlech-
ter. (Ibid., p. 249)

That becoming a human being does not begin until one withdraws
from the mass, this candid advice I would give to later generations.

(a) THE ATTEMPT TO ESCAPE

The Böll hero is isolated from those around him by a heightened
sensitivity. He has an awareness that separates him from the
insensitive majority, the 'others', and leaves him in isolation.
Andreas, *Der Zug war pünktlich*, obsessed by the impossibility
of avoiding death, is so much in the grip of fear that he has lost
all objective points of reference. Time and space are measured
only by when and where he is to die. It is the awareness of
death, his *sensitivity* to the human condition, that separates
him from the unaware whose vision is limited to and by
material things.

1. Es wäre wahnsinnig schwer, mit den anderen allein zu
sein, die jetzt den Flur füllen, diesen Schwätzern, die von
nichts reden können als von Urlaub und Heldentum, von
Beförderungen und Orden, von Fressen und von Tabak
. . . (*Der Zug war pünktlich*, p. 37)

It would be dreadfully difficult to be alone with the others who now
fill the corridor, with these idle chatterers who can speak of nothing
but leave, heroism, promotion, medals, eating, tobacco . . .

Greck too, *Wo warst du, Adam?*, sensitive and totally un-
suited to the life he must lead, is isolated from his fellow-
soldiers, ill at ease in the world he has to inhabit. On impulse,
he takes a ride in a swing-boat. He is able to escape, if only for
a few moments, from the confines of the material world into a
world where other sanctions appear to apply. He sees everything from a different angle, unspoiled by 'normal' perspective;
he has a brief glimpse of reality.

2. Er wußte plötzlich, daß er etwas Wesentliches in seinem
   Leben versäumt hatte: Schiffsschaukel fahren. Das war ja
   herrlich . . . und außerdem: die Welt war verändert . . .
   Dann stand das Schiff, er wußte, daß er lächerlich und
   jämmerlich aussah . . . (*Wo warst du, Adam?*, pp. 52–3)

> He realized suddenly that he had missed an essential thing in his life:
> riding in a swing-boat. It was marvellous . . . and something more:
> the world was quite changed . . . Then the swing stopped, he knew
> that he looked pitiful and ridiculous . . .

Frau Brielach, equally ill-equipped for the loveless life she
has led since the death of her husband, seeks escape in the
cinema.

3. Am schönsten wäre es gewesen, ins Kino zu gehen: dort
   war es dunkel und warm und die Zeit schmolz so lau und
   schmerzlos dahin . . . Das Kino war gut and ruhig . . .
   (*Haus ohne Hüter*, pp. 36–7)

> It would have been best to go to the cinema: there it was dark and
> warm and time melted away softly and painlessly—the cinema was
> good and peaceful . . .

Fred Bogner is similarly ill at ease. He is inarticulate but
sensitive enough to realize in moments of vision that there is
something wrong with the material life the 'others', the well-
adjusted ones, the articulate conformists, unthinkingly accept.

4. . . . und es kamen Augenblicke, in denen ich glaubte, ich
   hätte recht und alle anderen unrecht, weil sie alle so
   schön zu reden verstanden, und ich fand nie Worte. (*Und
   sagte kein einziges Wort*, p. 145)

> . . . and there were moments when I believed that I was right and all
> the others were wrong because they knew how to express themselves
> and I never found words.

All are paralysed by the circumstances in which they find themselves. Aware but inarticulate, isolated from others, unable to act decisively, they seek escape from the pressures of the world without realizing why.

(*b*) CONSCIOUS WITHDRAWAL

Nella Bach and Walter Fendrich, more sophisticated than Frau Brielach and Fred Bogner, make a conscious decision to withdraw from life. Nella retreats into the past and into the future that might have been. Walter withdraws from the materialistic society and in moments of special awareness feels the beginning of that alienation which later characters choose as a way of life. Nella deliberately abandons the present, haunts the places she used to frequent with Rai, stimulates her memories.

1. Licht aus und auf den Knopf gedrückt, und der Traum, der dazu bestimmt gewesen war, Wirklichkeit zu werden, flimmerte über das Hirn hin. (*Haus ohne Hüter*, p. 25)

   Turn out the light, press the button and the dream that had been meant to become reality flickered across her brain.

She has become:

2. . . . eine Frau . . . die Träume einnimmt wie man Morphium schluckt, bewußt und gierig . . . (Ibid., p. 77)

   . . . a woman who swallows dreams like morphia, greedily, aware of the consequences . . .

Walter, in his flight from the materialistic society, ceases to exist. Completely divorced from his former self he appears to a friend like one who has committed suicide. He no longer recognizes himself.

3. . . . und inzwischen hatte ich vergessen, wer ich war, wie
ich aussah und welchen Beruf ich hatte. (*Das Brot der
frühen Jahre*, pp. 53–4)

> . . . meanwhile I had forgotten who I was, what I looked like and what
> my job was.

4. Und als ich unter den Scheck meinen Namen schrieb,
. . . kam ich mir vor wie jemand, der eine Scheckfälschung
begeht. (Ibid., p .54)

> And when I signed my name on a cheque I felt like someone com-
> mitting a forgery.

It is a period of confusion. It is a period divorced from time and
body, in which his brain functions with extraordinary clarity.

5. Mein Gehirn arbeitete weiter, wie eine Maschine, die
auszuschalten man vergaß . . . (Ibid., p. 61)

> My brain went on working like a machine somebody had forgotten
> to switch off . . .

6. . . . und zugleich war ich so wach, wie ich es nie gewesen
war . . . (Ibid., p. 62)

> . . . and at the same time I was more alert than I had ever been
> before . . .

This feeling of clarity, of arbitrary severance, of sovereign
command, is the basis on which the most sophisticated of
Böll's characters seek to live their lives as free agents.

(*c*) LIFE AS PLAY

The Fähmels, Heinrich, Robert and Johanna, consciously
decide not merely on passive withdrawal from life but on active
formulation of the way their life is to express itself. They are

determined to control events, to create myths, to look upon life as a game they can play according to their own rules.

Heinrich Fähmel, architect, son of a musician, sees his life in terms of a dance. He decides on the impression he wants to create and devotes his energies to that end. He projects the image he wishes others to see.

1. . . . gab ihnen zu sehen, was sie sehen sollten. (*Billard um halb zehn*, p. 68)

> . . . let them see what they ought to see.

2. Ich hatte mir Handlungen, Bewegungen, einen präzisen Tageslauf vorgeschrieben, von dem Augenblick an, da ich die Stadt betrat, eine komplizierte Tanzfigur entworfen, in der ich Solotänzer und Ballettmeister in einer Person war; Komparserie und Kulissen standen mir kostenlos zur Verfügung. (Ibid., p. 60)

> I had planned out my actions, movements, my whole daily routine from the moment I entered the city, I had created a complicated dance routine in which I was both the solo dancer and the choreographer; supporting players and backcloth were at my disposal.

He has planned out his whole future and delights in the game.

3. . . . ich wußte es, während ich dort stand, bereit den Tanz zu beginnen. (Ibid., p. 61)

4. . . . der Mythos, den ich begründen wollte, war schon im Entstehen begriffen . . . (Ibid., p. 67)

5. . . . ich liebte das Spiel . . . (Ibid., p. 85)

> . . . I knew, as I stood there, ready to begin the dance.
>
> . . . the myth I was going to create was already underway . . .
>
> . . . I adored the game . . .

He is the star player as well as the director. Other human beings are his own creation, puppets, supporting players in his production.

> 6. . . . gut geölte Gelenke hatten meine Komparsen, wurden von unsichtbaren Fäden bewegt, Münder öffneten sich zu Stichworten, die ich ihnen zugestand . . . (Ibid., p. 87)

>> . . . my supporting players had well-oiled limbs, were moved by invisible strings, mouths opened to issue the words which I put into them . . .

He observes, waits and watches, in ironic detachment.

His son, Robert, is a statistician. He too cultivates an image, dry, remote, devoid equally of human desires and human failings. Fascinated by formulae, he finds satisfaction in his daily game of billiards. Totally absorbed in the everchanging patterns he has reduced the perpetual change and movement of life to an intellectual abstraction.

> 7. . . . keine Gestalt und nichts Bleibendes, nur Flüchtiges, löschte sich im Rollen der Kugel wieder aus; oft spielte er halbe Stunden lang nur mit einem einzigen Ball; weiß über grün gestoßen, nur ein einziger Stern am Himmel; leicht, leise, Musik ohne Melodie, Malerei ohne Bild; kaum Farbe, nur Formel. (Ibid., p. 30)

>> . . . no shape, nothing permanent, only transitory images dissolved again in the rolling of the ball, often he played for half hours at a time with one single ball; white pushed across green, one single star in the sky; soft, light, music without melody, painting without a picture; hardly colour only formula.

Absorbed in his intellectual game he apprehends people not as human beings but as gesture and mannerism. He too is sovereign in his own world.

Johanna, Heinrich's wife, has withdrawn physically from life and her game is played out with time. Under the guise of insanity she manipulates time and space to suit herself. She sees herself as imprisoned in a kind of underworld, a bewitched castle.

8. . . . Schloß, in das ich verwünscht bin . . . nur durch riesige Leitern ist die Welt erreichbar . . . (Ibid., p. 104)

> . . . a castle in which I am held in a spell . . . the outside world can only be reached by huge ladders . . .

She is perfectly aware that it is a game she plays and is not taken in herself but she insists her son and husband play with her and do not force her to face reality. It is a game not without its dangers.

9. Vorsicht, sonst werde ich wirklich verrückt, wird das Spiel ernst, und ich falle in das ewige Heute endgültig zurück, finde die Schwelle nicht mehr, renne um die bewachsenen Mauern herum, ohne den Eingang zu finden . . . (Ibid., p. 204)

> Take care, otherwise I shall really go mad, the game will become real and I shall fall back into the eternal today, I'll never find the entrance again, I'll run round the overgrown walls and not find the entrance . . .

(d) COMPLETE ALIENATION. THE EXPERIENCE OF THE ABSURD

The technique of deliberate withdrawal and its consequent personal liberation is satisfactory until, abruptly, *das Spiel wird ernst*, the game becomes real. The individual loses control.

In Hans Schnier alienation is total. It is no longer escape, withdrawal or play; it is a *way of life*. In choosing to be a clown he has chosen to observe, to perform, to imitate rather than to be. He has taken the final step along a dangerous road. No one can understand him or make contact with him.

1. Man weiß ja nie, wo man mit dir dran ist! (*Ansichten eines Clowns*, p. 144)

   One never knows where one is with you.

He is alone, unsure of his identity, observing and being observed; he is both himself and everything outside himself.

2. Hinter meinen geschlossenen Lidern sah ich mein Gesicht . . . vollkommen unbewegt, schneeweiß geschminkt, nicht einmal die Wimpern bewegten sich . . . Ich war tot und auf tausend Stunden mit meinem Gesicht eingesperrt . . . (Ibid., p. 153)

   Behind my closed lids I saw my face . . . completely motionless, painted white, not even the eyelashes moved . . . I was dead and imprisoned with my face for endless hours . . .

There is no longer a clear line between what is real and what is play.

3. Ich kann einen Blinden so gut spielen, daß man glaubt, ich wäre blind. Ich kam mir auch blind vor, vielleicht würde ich blind bleiben. (Ibid. p. 154)

   I can pretend to be blind so well that they believe I am blind. I felt blind myself, perhaps I would stay blind.

Schnier stands nearer to Johanna than to Heinrich and Robert. He stands on the edge of madness—the clown, the fool. He sees everything in isolation for he collects fragmentary moments. As he sits alone in his flat in Bonn, connected only by telephone to the outside world, time and space are both relative to him, past and present equally distant. He is the centre, everything else is of importance only in its relationship to him. He is *the only point of reference*. Reality begins and ends in him. Without illusions, without ideals he sees all too clearly into the nature of reality. He refuses to form it subjectively into an ordered whole as we, the normal ones, do. *He sees objectively.* He sees the unrelated external world as the systemless chaos it is. He is quite *free* but quite *alone.*

D. Participation

Although Böll apprehends the world intellectually as Hans Schnier, his moral convictions will not allow this apprehension to overwhelm him. His sturdy, practical background comes to his aid. His reaction to the state in which modern humanity finds itself is summed up in the title of the short story *Es muß etwas geschehen. Entfernung*, negative dissociation, opting out to find personal freedom in isolation, is not only dangerous. It is simply not enough. Action must be taken. A fundamental change is needed in society and in the individual himself. Positive action is required.

(*a*) RECONCILIATION

A first step is reconciliation. The past must be faced, examined and absorbed. It must not be forgotten as Gäseler so casually asserts:

1. „Alles vergessen," sagte er, „systematisch meine Erinnerung geschlachtet. Man muß den Krieg vergessen." (*Haus ohne Hüter*, p. 169)

   'Forgotten everything,' he said, 'my memory systematically wiped clean. One has to forget the war.'

It must be faced if its lessons are to be learned. Albert takes Martin to see the place where Absalom Billig was kicked to death and he and Rai tortured. It is too dangerous to forget these things. To scatter forgetfulness over them is like scattering ash over slippery ice: the ice is still there and all the more dangerous for being covered up. Nella and Frau Brielach must escape from the photographs in which the past stands frozen if Heinrich and Martin, the innocent present, are to survive. Nella confronts the past in the person of Gäseler. To her surprise she discovers she cannot hate him—she merely finds him ridiculous and boring.

> 2. So sieht das Schicksal aus, so wie du: nicht düster, nicht grauenvoll, sondern wie du: langweilig. (Ibid., p. 164)
>
> So that's how fate looks, like you; not dark and menacing but like you, boring.

> 3. Haß kam nicht, nur Gähnen. (Ibid., p. 168)
>
> Hatred would not come only boredom.

Walter's hatred of Ulla's father dissolves when he turns to face his past.

> 4. . . . ich gab meinen Haß gegen ihn preis, wie ein Kind einen Luftballon, den es einen ganzen Sommersonntagnachmittag lang krampfhaft festgehalten hat—dann plötzlich losläßt, um ihn in den Abendhimmel steigen zu sehen, wo er kleiner wird, kleiner, bis er nicht mehr sichtbar ist. (*Das Brot der frühen Jahre*, pp. 67–8)
>
> . . . I let go my hatred for him as a child suddenly lets go a balloon which he has clutched convulsively all through a whole summer Sunday afternoon and sees floating away into the evening sky, where it becomes smaller and smaller, until it's no longer visible.

Both extremes, deliberately forgetting past events on the one hand and being obsessed by hatred for them on the other, are negative. The eating of Heinrich Fähmel's birthday cake, made

in the form of the abbey which has played an important role in
the life of the Fähmel family, symbolizes reconciliation as the
past is absorbed into the present.

(b) ACTION

The quiet absorbtion of the past is in its turn insufficient. It
merely clears the field for positive, present actions, for public
protest. Leo's sabotage of communications *Als der Krieg
ausbrach* is a gesture of defiance which costs him his life but he
has made his contribution, his moral protest. Johanna Fähmel,
although she feels safe in her enchanted castle, enclosed in past
time, does not hesitate to act when the time is ripe.

1. . . . der Herr spricht: „mein ist die Rache", aber warum
   soll ich nicht des Herren Werkzeug sein? (*Billard um halb
   zehn*, p. 117)

   . . . the Lord says: Vengeance is mine but why should I not be his
   instrument?

She fires the shot, not at her personal enemy in private vengeance but at the smooth enemy of society, not at Nettlinger
but at the Minister.

2. . . . nicht Tyrannenmord, sondern Anständigenmord—
   der Tod wird das große Staunen in sein Gesicht zurück-
   bringen . . . (Ibid., p. 215)

   . . . not against tyranny but against the upright 'decent' politician—
   death will bring back the capacity for wonder to his face . . .

Both these gestures are for humanity: Leo makes his against
the inhumanity of war, Johanna against the inhumanity of a
society[1] which has forgotten how to feel and how to grieve.

---

[1] cf. Paul, '*Im Tal der donnernden Hufe*', p. 63.

3. ... anständig, anständig und keine Spur von Trauer im
   Gesicht: was ist ein Mensch ohne Trauer? (Ibid., p. 212)

   ... decent, respectable, not a trace of grief in their faces. What is a
   human being without the capacity for grief?

The tragedy of society is not so much that the *Büffel* exist but
that so few are willing to protest against them. Schrella to
Robert:

4. ... ich seh sie da unten ... Nettlinger, Wakeira, ich habe
   nicht Angst, weil es die da unten gibt, sondern weil es die
   anderen nicht gibt ... (Ibid., p. 227)

   ... I see them down there ... I am not worried because they exist
   but because the others do not ...

Even Robert, remote, withdrawn, free, could fulfil an active
role in society: that of shepherd for the lambs. They need guidance and protection.

5. „Ich werde nicht können," sagte ich, „ich kann nicht
   Lamm sein."

   „Hirten," sagte er, „es gibt welche, die die Herde nicht
   verlassen." (Ibid., p. 39)

   'I cannot,' I said, 'I cannot be a lamb.'
   'Shepherds,' he said, 'there are some who do not abandon the flock.'

That he is suited to such a service is made clear by Marianne.

6. ... ich fühle mich geschützt in seiner Nähe. (Ibid., p.
   220)

   ... I feel protected when I am near him.

His adoption of Hugo, *das Lamm Gottes*, symbolizes his active acceptance of his social obligations.

In his most recent novel *Ende einer Dienstfahrt*, a book reminiscent of *Irisches Tagebuch* in its gaiety and charm, the younger Gruhl deserts from the Army. He too is opting out of a ridiculous machine. But desertion is too negative a form of protest. With the help of his father he creates a 'happening'; he sets fire to the jeep he was driving. The Gruhls are not revolutionaries. They are honest, sensible, practical men.

7. Die beiden wirkten gesund . . . sauber und ruhig; sie wirkten nicht nur gefaßt sondern heiter. (*Ende einer Dienstfahrt*, p. 12)

   They struck everyone as healthy . . . clean and peaceful; they were not only composed but serenely happy.

They are Böll's *selige Asozialen*, happy outsiders, contented with their lives but prepared to make the grand gesture as a *natural* action, without fear or remorse.

8. Vom Vorsitzenden gefragt, ob sie Reue empfänden, antworteten beide ohne Zögern und ohne Einschränkung mit „Nein". (Ibid., p. 17)

   Asked by the Court whether they regretted their action they both answered unhesitatingly and without prevarication 'No'.

To themselves, their reasons are good enough. They are content to have struck a blow for common sense, for humanity, against a cold insensitive society.

9. Wir froren ein bißchen und wollten uns durch ein Häppening aufwärmen (Ibid., p. 24)

   We were rather cold and wanted to warm ourselves up with a happening.

To sum up: The concern of Böll for *die Bewältigung der Vergangenheit,* the coming to terms with the past, has its effect on both the form and content of the novels. This is his major theme and forms the basis for his criticism of contemporary society. The creation of a humane society should be the concern of every individual and will not be achieved by withdrawal and preoccupation with self. Active participation is essential if a new society, one that will offer *Die Chance des Humanen,* is to emerge.

Conclusions in Brief

Böll und fünfzig, düster, was? weil man doch oft überhaupt nichts hört von ihm, nie sagt er was, und dann
plötzlich . . . wieder zu viel . . . der kann sich überhaupt
nicht beherrschen . . . da bin ich viel ruhiger, ich bin
richtig froh, wenn ich höre, Böll ist für eine Zeit wieder in
Irland . . . (Martin Walser: *In Sachen Böll*, p. 312)

> Böll at fifty, a grim thought? Often one hears absolutely nothing
> from him, he never says anything and then suddenly he says too much
> again . . . he is quite unable to control himself . . . so I am much
> less on edge, I am really quite happy when I hear Böll is in Ireland
> again for a time . . .

This is Martin Walser's judgment on Böll in middle age—
sentiments which must be echoed by many of Böll's contemporaries. West German society can breathe freely for a
while—Böll, her constant critic, is temporarily out of the way.

To his critics Böll is a tiresome creature who has not realized
that the war is over and that West Germany is now a highly
successful, accepted member of the European community, its
inhabitants reinstated and prosperous. He refuses to see that
everything is now splendidly in order. His preoccupation with
the war and its aftermath, with the Nazi régime, with the past,
dates him and makes of him a recorder of past events. He is like
an ageing knight tilting at the same dismal windmills, refighting
old campaigns, always dissatisfied and frequently turning on
those who pay him the compliment of asking for his views. His
speech at the *Woche der Brüderlichkeit* (1970) would seem to
substantiate this.

To some he appears a destructive critic with few constructive ideas. He attacks church organization, talks of love, compassion and humanity without being specific as to how the church is to function. It must, after all, have a form. Similarly it remains unclear when he attacks the state and society just what sort of concept he has of them.

> Undeutlich ist mir geblieben, was für eine Art Staat Ihnen insgeheim vor Augen steht . . . (Dolf Sternberger: *In Sachen Böll*, p. 135)
>
> I am still far from clear as to what sort of state you visualize . . .

He demands a *rahmenlose Gesellschaft*, but as one critic points out:

> Eine „rahmenlose Gesellschaft" ist eine Schwärmerei. (Dolf Sternberger: *Böll bleibt in Rahmen*, 18 March 1970)
>
> A society without any kind of framework is a delusion.

To some extent these criticisms are justified. But they are superficial. The contribution of Böll to contemporary literature is far greater than that of a mere recorder or a soured critic. His work is not a chronicle of German history 1943–70. It is an assessment of the nature of existence and an attempt to solve the dilemma of man within the framework of contemporary society.

Böll is preoccupied with the war because for him it was a *crisis*. He experienced it as a revelation of the chaotic nature of existence. It was not merely a clash between opposing armies but a *manifestation of the permanent confrontation between abstract power*, brutal and uncompromising, *and human life*. The sinister aspect of this became clear to him when the end of the war, the economic miracle, the betterment of material conditions, did not alter the basic situation. Böll realized, after a brief period of fruitless hope, that all that had taken place, was a metamorphosis of the brutality, stupidity and power of war into that of state and society. The position of the individual human being remained unchanged. He was as insignificant in a society geared to organisation and productivity as he had been in a society geared to war. The war therefore was not an isolated experience of a senseless conflict; it was a manifestation of the chaos that lurks perpetually behind the world as we perceive it. As the physical world disintegrated around him he realized he had seen it for the first time in its natural state: *a confusion of unrelated phenomena, unreasonable, inexplicable and incomprehensible.* As such, it presents itself to the isolated human consciousness and that consciousness alone gives it the only cohesion it possesses. It has no inherent meaning. Existence itself emerges from the experience of total war as disconcertingly *grotesque, irrational* and *absurd.*

When confronted by a revelation of such enormity, clear-cut definitions of the physical structure of the ideal society or of the exact form the Church should adopt, are trivial and superficial. The fundamental fact is the situation in which the isolated human being finds himself *vis-à-vis* the inimical world; the basic question is how can he live a meaningful life in a meaningless world. Böll quickly rejects his initial solution: the resolving of all isolation in death where a final meaning is found. This would hardly be a solution for life and the living. Similarly he rejects withdrawal into individual freedom, seeing this as an acerbation of the basic problem of isolation. Hence his final solution: *active participation* in the *preservation* of *die Würde des Menschen,*[1] *the dignity of man.* Respect for the individual gives meaning and dignity to life, and dignity alone makes human life of value. If society and Church devote themselves to this end they will discover their necessary form. Form comes at the end, not at the beginning. It must be worked for and will

[1] cf. p. 37, Quote 2.

be right if the priorities of content are right. We are all work-men, we are all involved in the fashioning of a humane society and a loving Church. In *participation*, in the *communication* with, and the *service* of, others towards mutual betterment and fulfilment lies the salvation of the individual, the possibility of life as opposed to a living death. We are all concerned in 'an augmentation of the possibilities of loving' which must lead to a satisfying and integrated existence.

> Der Brief an uns ist geschrieben, die Aufgabe ist gestellt, die Schlüssel bekommen wir überreicht: . . . es geht auf Leben und Tod. (*Hierzulande*, pp. 66–7)

> The letter is addressed to us, the task is set, we are given the keys .. . it is a matter of life and death

Bibliography

A. Chronological list of works by Heinrich Böll referred to in this book

Der Zug war pünktlich, 1949, Ullstein Bücher 415.

Wanderer, kommst du nach Spa . . ., Short Stories, 1947–50, D.T.V. 437.

Wo warst du, Adam? 1951, Ullstein Bücher 84.

Nicht nur zur Weihnachtszeit, Satires, 1951–61, D.T.V. 350.

Hierzulande Aufsätze zur Zeit, Essays, 1952–61, D.T.V. 11.

Und sagte kein einziges Wort, 1953, Ullstein Bücher 141.

Zum Tee bei Dr Borsig, Hörspiele 1953–63, D.T.V. 200.

Haus ohne Hüter, 1954, Ullstein Bücher 185.

Das Brot der frühen Jahre, 1955, Ullstein Bücher 239.

Irisches Tagebuch, 1957, D.T.V. 1.

Billard um halb zehn, 1959, Knaur 8.

Als der Krieg ausbrach, Stories, 1950–64, D.T.V. 339.

Ansichten eines Clowns, 1963, D.T.V. 400.

Entfernung von der Truppe, 1964, D.T.V. 339.

Frankfurter Vorlesungen, 1964, D.T.V. 68.

Ende einer Dienstfahrt, 1966, D.T.V. 566.

Aufsätze Kritiken Reden, 1952–67, Kiepenheuer und Witsch 1967.

A complete bibliography of the works of Heinrich Böll and all relative secondary literature is given in:

Der Schriftsteller Heinrich Böll: biographisch—bibliographischer Abriss, D.T.V. 530.

D.T.V., Deutscher Taschenbuch Verlag.

116   A STUDENT'S GUIDE TO BÖLL

B. A selection of recommended critical literature on Heinrich Böll

Beckel, Albrecht: *Mensch, Gesellschaft, Kirche bei Heinrich Böll*. Mit einem Beitrag von Heinrich Böll: Interview mit mir selbst. Osnabruck: Fromm 1966.

Berger, K. H.: *Heinrich Böll*. In *Schriftsteller der Gegenwart*. Berlin: Volk und Wissen Volkseigener Verlag 1967.

Jeziorkowski, Klaus: *Rhythmus und Figur*. Zur Technik der epischen Konstruktion in Heinrich Bölls, *Der Wegwerfer* und *Billard um halb zehn*. Bad Homburg v.d.H.: Gehlen 1968.

Schwarz, Wilhelm Johann: *Der Erzähler Heinrich Böll*. Seine Werke und Gestalten. Bern, München: Franke 1967.

Stresau, Hermann: *Heinrich Böll*. Berlin: Coloquium Verlag 1964 (Köpfe des XX Jahrhunderts Bd. 33).

Wirth, Günter: *Heinrich Böll*. Essayistische Studie über religiöse und gesellschaftliche Motive im Prosawerk des Dichters. Berlin: Union Verlag 1967.

Individual Stories

Interpretationen zu Heinrich Böll. Kurzgeschichten I and II. München: R. Oldenbourg Verlag, München 1965.

Articles

Reid, J. H.: *Time in the Works of Heinrich Böll*. In *Modern Language Review*, Vol 62, No. 3 (July 1967), pp. 476–85.

Waidson, H. M.: *The Novels and Stories of Heinrich Böll*. In *German Life and Letters*. NS No. 4 (July 1959), pp. 264–72.

Zielkowski, Theodore: *Albert Camus and Heinrich Böll*. In *Modern Language Notes*. Baltimore 77, pp. 282–91.

C. General Background

Pascal, Roy: *The German Novel*. Manchester U.P. 1956.

Thomas, R. Hinton and van der Will, Wilfried: *The German Novel and the Affluent Society*. Manchester U.P. 1968.

Waidson, Herbert Morgan: *The Modern German Novel*. O.U.P. 1959.